This Journey We Call Running

Early Reviews

"The poem, *Inside the Run*, was a flashback for me; what it was like to run, to get everything right, by being among the few out there early in the morning. The short stories, poems and reflections in *This Journey We Call Running*, help to get me back to that pure sense of why I run, race and what I want it to mean in my life."

- Tony Schiller, Race Director, Speaker.
7-time Triathlon Age-Group World Champion

"For all of us who enjoy running as more than just training to race; Brian Siddons, through poetry and prose in his book, *This Journey We Call Running*, captures the lifetime enjoyment of running as a process that can begin over and over again. I especially enjoyed the poem, *For Gabe*. It captured her spirit in running and her too short life."

-Gloria Jansen, Certified Running Coach.
Nationally recognized Age-Group Runner

Comments from runners with an early preview.

"Awesome Brian!! Thanks for sharing!"

Tim S.

"Absolutely beautiful <3 Thank you!!!"

Stacy E.

"I'm going to save this and read it as the week passes! Beautiful."

Lynnette G.-C.

"So BEAUTIFUL, brother🎳 gonna print this out and put it on my fridge🖤"

Ron R.

"Keeping a self-copy thank you."

Benjamin H.

"What a beautiful poem. I love it!"

Lori E.-R.

"Awesome fantastic wonderful!!!!!! Thank you so much!!!! I have a tough 50k trail run this Saturday! So appropriate!!!!"

Doug H.

"Darn. I think I'm going to cry."

Vasantha B.

"Beautiful! You are obviously a gifted poet. You've captured us completely!"

Helen S.

"Oye! Bravo! Ok, that is beautiful!"

Rose B.

"You put into words so eloquently what I am feeling. Thank you!"

Laine M.

"Oh, that is brilliant, thank you!"

Sharyn M.

THIS JOURNEY WE CALL RUNNING

THIS JOURNEY WE CALL RUNNING

ONE RUNNER'S ANTHOLOGY

Brian James Siddons

Brian James Siddons

July 10, 2021

To Excel In Life
Andover, MN

Published in the United States
by
To Excel In Life
Andover, Minnesota

Cover Photo by: Harrison Siddons
Author Photo by: Harrison Siddons
Book Design by: Brian James Siddons

BrianJamesSiddons.com

Library of Congress Control Number: 2019909456

ISBN   978-0-578-53938-6

Printed in the United States

First Edition

Dedicated to
my brother, Al.

Mentor,
teacher,
coach,
friend.

Thank you for the
introduction to running
and the lifelong
example you have set by
always giving your best.

Foreword

Brian Siddons can't run without writing, and he's been running for 45 years, so his new book *This Journey We Call Running* is overflowing with rhythms and emotions we have all encountered. His personal essays and poems capture the essence of running, the good days and the challenging. You've been there many times yourself; Siddons has conveniently captured the moments for you.

I particularly enjoyed his rumination on the similarities between Sir James Dyson, inventor of supercharged vacuum cleaners, and many marathoners. Life throws plenty of roadblocks our way; we succeed when we persist and go even harder. In an essay titled "Magic Legs & Fluid Pens," Siddons explains that "trusting in the process" is the key to our continued striving. Of course, I nodded in agreement with his "Ode to One Last Race," which must, of course, start out in "Hopkinton way."

You'll also find much to appreciate in this modest collection. In fact, you'll surely find yourself turning back to read and reread Siddons's most evocative pieces.

Amby Burfoot
1968 Boston Marathon winner
Longtime Runner's World editor and writer
Author, most recently, of *Run Forever*

Stick to the Plan

Like running, writing is a task of many small steps. Eventually, most writing will lead to a story, or a poem, or even a novel. Such was my case in the origin of this book. Upon receiving more and more positive feedback from runners, I decided it was time for me to start in on the arduous work of putting out a book.

With the support of my wife, Jeanette, and encouragement by my running friends, family and others that have read my work along the way, I put together a schedule like any good runner would do and started training, I mean, editing.

The journey that brought this book to its finish line is one that I will cherish. It wouldn't have happened without the help and support of so many.

Special thanks to Jeanette and our children and their significant others; Jackie and Bill, Spencer and Liz, Harrison and Zoey. Thank you for the unconditional support and love. You are my true inspiration in life!

Al and Bev, thank you for your encouragement.

Running crew Stan and Dave, aka Laser & Beast! You guys prop me up like no other. Running Brothers!

World Class guidance and support from Amby and Geoff provided the extra confidence I needed at just the right time to see this through to the finish. Thank you!

To all that have cheered me on with your kind words and expressions of how my writing has made an impact on you...the feeling is mutual. You have fueled me to keep up the pace, and I will be forever grateful to you!
#BostonBuddies
#RunningOver60

The Team

It has been a joy to share all the aspects of what it takes to complete a book, and I'm grateful to have so much support. We had originally planned for a group of runners on the cover, but in the end decided on a solo shot. My thanks to everyone that participated in our original photo shoot at Bunker Hills Regional Park, where I get in most of my training miles, it was a fun morning. Although they didn't make the cover, I couldn't pass up including this great picture of the team!

Zoey, Harrison, Jackie, Theo, Bill, Dave, Henry, Mary, Brian, Jeanette, Kevin, Etta, Stan, Todd.

Photo credit: Harrison Siddons

Contents

THIS JOURNEY WE CALL RUNNING

Run as One

Patterned treads leave traces
Of a runner's steady gait.
Encrusted upon snow covered asphalt paths.
Dug into the soft earth of forested trails.
Printed in disappearing ink down the puddled sidewalks.

Well before the suns pink glow
Banks it's glory off thin clouds spread
Endlessly across the sky,
The tribe traces dotted lines
Throughout the landscape
While most of the slowly awakening
Populace remain nestled in bed.

Like the pleasant sighting of a doe
Snacking on flora in the park,
Those in varying modes of transit
To work, on errand or otherwise
Out and about early upon the roads,
May round a corner or crest a bridge
And feel inspired by the lean silhouette
Of a long-distance runner moving
In well-rehearsed rhythm.

What appears as a two-legged loner,
Is in truth a multi-headed beast.
Driven by an inner desire to improve,
Fueled with a passion for competition,
Each runner draws faithfully upon the
Power of the tribe to sustain their effort,
Channeling the far-reaching
Attributes of the tribe.

Boundless energy,
Shared compassion,
We've-got-you support and
Unconditional acceptance.

Though alone, each runner
Is focused, their mind brimming with
Thoughtful encouragements and
Heartfelt guidance from the tribe.
Experiences of hard-earned successes
and goal-oriented breakthroughs
of so many in the tribe are recalled.
The lone runner responds.
Faster, tougher, more confident.

Running together, alone.
Running alone, together.
Running.
Running.
Forever running as one.

Magic Legs and Fluid Pen

Runners, like writers, have good days and not so good days. We have runs that are called grinders because it takes all we've got to grind out a few average training miles.

Writers know this same feeling. Once beyond the dreaded "block", or as runners say, once out the door, you can be ready to write page upon page and yet the pen, full of ink, dares you to make a mark on the page. The grip feels awkward, your chair off kilter, the lighting too dim. And yet, after the cursory prep, the writing, as rough and chunky as it may be, is begun. You finish, in a time longer than expected, and are quite glad to turn the tablet to a fresh page for tomorrows effort.

On the morrow, the sun rises within minutes of the previous day's peak above the horizon. My routine for a morning run remains the same and I am out the door headed on a familiar route like so many days before.

I tear down my street already feeling good. I won't look at my GPS watch for fear of finding I've started too quickly and will soon burn out, regretting my decision to let my mood dictate what should be a monitored effort.

The tar of the bike path feels softer today as my legs respond to the pace with an ease that tells me I'm in for a treat. Breathing is neither labored nor easy. Somewhere between just rapid enough and not so insane that I sound like I'm gasping to survive.

By mile two I'm committed to the effort of "running with fatigue". I make a deal with my body like I'm talking with a coach.

Me: "I'll keep this pace, but I'll need to cut the mileage from eight to six miles."

Mind Coach: "No way, you need this workout to improve your endurance. Seven miles minimum!"

Me: "I know, and I've got to take advantage of how I feel. My body is flowing like I'm being pushed by the wind. My breathing is less labored than during my track workouts and my legs feel really fresh after a rest day."

Mind Coach: "Then it's settled. Seven miles as fast as you can maintain."

I agree to run with the fatigue I know will make me stronger. "I'll do it", I say, and I must, for today the magic legs are back!

Mile four clicks off and I begin to unleash my body for the last three miles. Mile five is a blur of effort, pain and joy as I prep for the last mile before the last mile.

Arms working, body mechanics constantly in check for alignment. The sound of my feet pushing off the grit of dust and sand on the asphalt path remind me of running on the track, the place where speed is honed as we push ourselves as hard as we can. I feel like I'm flying the last mile, daring myself to go as fast as I can and still remain able to gas it all the way back to the finish line I call my driveway.

These benchmark runs are few and far between, and yet come at just the right intervals. After weeks of hard work, these paydays arrive, and I cash the check without hesitation. Like a great session of writing, it feeds me for days, sometimes longer, between the daily grind of everyday results.

Trusting in the process enables me to keep the faith that magic legs, and a fluid pen, are the blessings of cumulative efforts. Chipping away each day, resting when needed to freshen up the physical and mental self and then jumping back in with abandonment are the constants that prepare us for that moment when great things can happen.

Little Things that Humble

It's funny how things can sneak up on you. A little lack of focus, or maybe just paying lots of attention to something else when suddenly a new ailment, or work situation, or relationship has a "blister". Most of the time we can resolve these issues quickly, but not always. For me, it's these little things I miss that hit home and humble me the most. Mainly because they are usually preventable.

My latest slice of humble pie was served up during the winter for an ailment on my toes that looked like blisters but didn't hurt like a blister would. Maybe it was frostbite, kinda looked like the early stages of frostbite. It also looked like poison ivy; wrong season. Living in Minnesota, there are plenty of cold winter runs to deal with so the sooner I figure this out the better.

Time to check the internet about my toes. Chilblains, a pretty well-known ailment due mainly to a lack of circulation and or warming up the toes too quickly after being in the cold, was the clear winner in Name That Ailment. The docs suggest exercise...is running in the cold oxy-moronic when you have Chilblains? Most people may think it's just plain moronic, and maybe it is, a little. But, so far, my toes are getting better with me paying more attention to keeping all the little piggy's warm. Rubbing warming lotion on a couple of times a day helped.

As runners, we are often cruising along in our training. Running five days a week, mileage steady, and of course planning for future events. We schedule some early season races, some race-training halfs, and certainly talk about the marathon we are peaking for. Then, Chilblains, or some minor thing that says, "Hey, don't forget about me, your friend, Mr. Humble". And humbled we are, pulled off the course to attend to something new, something unexpected.

It's a great challenge, and one to expect. Fortunately, especially as we age, the training we do equips us to battle back, time and again. It takes a tremendous adversity for a DNF, and that's why the little things make me pay attention. Clear it up when it's small and manageable. Let it nag or become chronic and we're out of commission for weeks, or more.

I don't mind the little things anymore, they keep me humbled, and that's a good thing.

**"More than a habit, running is a cleansing,
a purification process that wrings out
stress and makes room for confidence."
#IAlwaysFeelBetterAfterIRun**
-BJSiddons

New Batteries

Tomorrow night I'll need to put in fresh, new batteries into my headlamp, for the third time this season. It's an odd benchmark of winter running, but also a badge of honor. It's been a blessing to have a group to train with this cycle, it really helps to get out the door when you know someone is meeting you on the corner at 5:15 a.m., even though you're not sure what the run holds in store.

That's also the beauty of it, never being able to predict what will happen, even for what appears to be another simple morning run, or another simple, 24-hour cycle of life. Both are quite the endeavor, but some days they can be almost automatic and hard to recall.

Running, and life, can also be filled with one or more of life's variables; challenging, exciting, sad, tough, wonderful, and more. On those days we work harder to make them count, to make them memorable. We want to engage those moments and live them as fully as possible.

As runners, we strive to master the essentials of daily life in the same manner we approach our craft. Relishing easy days yet doing our best to reach the goals we set. After a tough day, we don't roll over, we rise and move forward; optimistic our next run, our next day, will be more rewarding, more productive. At the end to a great day, we are grateful for the good fortune, no matter how hard we worked for it.

And every so often, as an extra little push, we get to put in some fresh, new batteries and hit the road again. Eager to take on a fresh, new day!

Free as the Wind

Through me, as if
I were made of linen.
Warm wind cleansing
Months of icy winter from my soul.

Embracing Mother Nature and
Her ever changing wonders,
Clad in the simplicity of
Distance-runner gear.
Feather-light cap shades the
Eyes that guide my way.
Knit poly, wrapped loose and light
Upon my ever-thinning torso.
Feet nestled upon a bed of
Comfort and cushion,
Softly bound by woven nylon.

Clarity and focus, perfect partners,
Fully engaged for another session.
Energized by the warmth of
Solar rays upon my skin.
Motivation filling my heart
As I envision reaching goals
So recently out of my grasp.

This is my favorite time,
Morning dawn or evening set,
The golden hour of the day.
All other pieces of life lay aside,
For the moment, of no matter to me.
I'm lost within the run, and yet,
I find my true self,
Each and every time.

It's the rush of life on a run.
Oxygen-depleted blood,
Fighting to get through veins.
Lungs exchanging less and less air,
Gasping more deeply each mile.
Muscles aching under the load,
Sinewy strands holding me together.
Heart pumping the pace in beats,
Chambers filling faster and faster.

I strive to humble myself on the good days,
I learn much about myself of the tough days.
The mornings I'd rather miss,
So often are the runs of pure joy.
The nights I'm so easy to sway,
Turn frequently into a sweaty success.

And on those lucky days,
Most times when I least expect,
The joy of pure running emerges.
Overtaking my struggle,
A calmness so transcendent,
I become the run.
Consciously unconscious.
Breaking into my forever stride,
A motion that feels no pain or effort,
I know it's time to let everything go, and,
For as long as I am able,
Run with such abandonment
I become utterly lost, and yet,
Completely rediscovered!

Your Pace or Mine

It's nice to have training partners. More than someone to run with a few days a week, a training partner keeps you honest all week long, and may or may not be headed for the same goal as you are. The trick is finding how to balance training efforts that fit into everyone's pace calculator. It's tough.

My wife, Jeanette, and I run together quite a bit, this past year especially, and it was very enjoyable. We made it through most of the Minnesota winter outdoors (only 83" of snow this past winter) and set our goal on the Medtronic Twin Cities Marathon (MTCM) in October. We trained with two other regulars during the winter who were also training for MTCM, and picked up another about mid-July. Our goal times were all over the place. From three hours for Bryan to 3:39 as my goal to 3:55 for Jeanette. "Under four" for Dave and Ben, and finally, for Stan, "to finish". It was going to be the first marathon for Dave, Ben and Stan.

Running as a group is such a fantastic way to train, but with such different time goals we couldn't all train together each session. The beauty of group running is that you can adjust your workouts to fit when it's best to run with the group. Bryan would hit his hard days with other, faster runners and use his group time for moderate and recovery runs. I could run hard with him on days that were tough for me, yet he would benefit from these as medium days. I'd do the same with Jeanette, running hard on my own or with Bryan, and with her for my medium days. For long runs, we'd all start together and just string out as the run progressed. We knew ahead of time the long runs would be a true compromise. Some days you had to run a bit slower or faster than you'd like, but the benefit of a training partner was well worth the tradeoff.

Jeanette and I had our best summer of running in a long time. Having each other, plus our training partners, was the biggest reason for our success. Friends to run with is the easiest way to get out the door and get a run done. It's fun, social, and motivating!

I'm very grateful for our training group. Give it a try, you'll be amazed at how much more you will enjoy your training and the increased fitness level you will attain.

**"Running in a race is simply one long game
of *Catch Me if You Can*. Just a little more organized."
#RunForFun**
-BJSiddons

A Run a Day Keeps the Doctor Away

I function so much better when I'm running consistently. Life, work, relationships...everything ebbs and flows in a more manageable manner. Not to say it's perfect but running enables me to handle challenges better. I feel more in touch and on top of things physically, mentally and spiritually.

It's a blessing to be able to run and train and I try not to take it for granted. Occasional injuries and setbacks over the years come and go, however my current stretch of about two years of consistent running is bearing some fresh fruit. Well, at this point in my life maybe I should say well-aged fruit, but it is nice to have a couple of years of training in the bank, and a bit of weight loss to boot.

As winter approaches, it will be tougher to get out the door and run. Darkness, cold temps and having to be more careful on the running paths due to snow and ice are recurring seasonal challenges. As does happen, things will slow down, but that's a trend of nature I don't mind settling in with for a few months. The craving my body, mind and spirit have for time outdoors needs the nourishment that, for me, only an hour or two of running down a winter path shadowed by pines and oaks, laden with snow, can fulfill.

Whether a morning start or a late evening finish, the exchange of cold, crisp air through my lungs begins the transformation that allows my soul to calm and my body to renew. While running may not be the answer for every person, a daily dose of a few miles is the one prescription I would wholeheartedly recommend to anyone.

Race Day Renewal

Anxiously awaiting the start,
Prepared for months in advance.
Excitement gives way to doubt,
If only temporarily, replaced by
Confidence in my abilities, in my goal.
Race day is coming,
I am ready.

Acknowledging the pain of effort,
Having met so frequently in training,
I swallow quickly to avoid the taste.
Fueled by desire in my heart and
Tenacity in my spirit,
Passion emerges and
Brings me through
Each struggle along the course.

Time and distance matter not,
For there is always
Someone faster,
Someone running further.
The challenge is to our self;
New goals, new adventures.

A final push brings me
Across the finish line.
Spent, weary, and
Smiling from ear to ear.
I cannot wait to
Relive, retell and regale the
Story of this race with
Family and friends.

I am energized, not tired,
I am invigorated, not beat down, as
The elixir of life flows strong within.
My runners pulse fills my
Soul with joy and elation, and yet, an
Overwhelming calm that only
Total exhaustion can deliver
Assures me I will not burst.

Post-race I am renewed,
Cleansed from within.
Baptized once again,
Into life as a runner.

A Dose of Progress

Progress sneaks up on us runners. Little bits of improvement sprinkled among the myriad of workouts. Hard pressed to notice day to day, incremental gains hide as we are distracted during our runs by things like how tough it is to breathe, that our shoes are feeling like cardboard, or why does this hill seem steeper today?

We consume ourselves with the present, which is how we improve our focus, yet the rudimentary benefits of training go un-noticed even after a few weeks of solid sessions. Improvements are not something that is able to jump up and wave at us like a spectator on the sidelines. We know faster days are out there, like a cautious deer in a nearby woods, hunkered down and surrounded by tall prairie grass.

Then one day, we show up on the route a little early and surprise the doe that again has waited patiently for us to pass by at our normal hour. Today, we've started early and our course is run with a bit more enthusiasm. Faster early pace, steady longer in the middle and then a wonderful finish that we're able to maintain to the rusty mailbox that marks the end of our runs. We flourish on this day and then we look at each other like, "Where did that come from?"

I've watched my children and their teammates in sports for many years, even coached for a number of them, and each year it's the same. Shaky start, fun during the season, and a nice finish. It's hard to see from practice to practice, game to game, but improvement happens. Add in a little faith, a little positive attitude and a dose of confidence and suddenly their efforts yield great results.

Not every season brings a PR or a championship, but every season is a chance to experience something new, something memorable. Step by step, we can all get there.

Winter Reflection:
The Gift of Running with Friends

Winter has finally arrived, at least for a few days here in Minnesota, making this New Year's Day run with friends one to remember. The trails were tricky enough due to the previous evening's rain and snow. Adding in brisk gusts of 20-mph winds on a 14-degree day made for a bit of a battle on the way back home. It was good to run with others today, and especially good to see Jeanette get in a five-mile run, her first at this distance since taking time off for a post-marathon injury. Bryan, Dave and I got in nine miles, the weather making it feel like 15 in the hills.

With all its seasonal extras, winter really is a great time to ease back the training into moderate-pace mode. During our workouts we can talk more easily, discussing topics that are less about training and more about life. Of course, we still dream about spring running; the warm weather, the clear trails and, if we stay healthy, faster workouts and race goals.

But we love winter running. There is a purity and beauty in the park when it's covered in snow. Daytime runs, with a sunny sky, remind me of being in the mountains. Pine, oak and spruce trees coated in snow. Fields of tall bushes and prairie grass disappearing under natures protective blanket. Tracks of wildlife and Nordic skiers across the trails. On our evening runs, when the clouds reflect the city lights back down onto the snow, we can turn off our headlamps and run through the park without artificial light. It's one of my favorite times of the year for a workout.

Running through winter, bundled in extra gear and treading lightly on ice and snow laden trails, gives me the gift of slowing down to savor the journey that is training with my run crew, keeping me warm on even the coldest of days.

Getting Out the Door

One ear, uncovered,
receives the echoes that have filtered through
separate lines of defense:
the wet, colonial blue siding,
the window of double pane strength,
the lowly flowered curtain.

Silent, miniature water bombs
explode onto the cedar plank deck.
Pure h2o droplets splashdown into the still uncovered
above ground pool.
Streams of liquid life pour off the roof and
waterfall onto the river rock below.
My bedroom is alive with the vibrato of
natures great gift of rain.

Can't think, must act without stopping to
ponder the options.
Down the stairs, using the glow from my
cell phone to light each step.
Labrador following, ready for food, cat clawing the
table post, stretching herself awake.
I lumber to the mudroom after a pitstop,
thankful for a fresh set of togs.

It's fall, and cold mornings are made even less pleasant by
the late arrival of the sunrise.
As I finish getting ready,
light from a single room leaks into the now quiet kitchen.
I see by the clock more time has slipped by
than I had planned.
I will trade back the minutes by
eating breakfast at work today.

The cold air hits me first,
with hints of suburbia tossed into the wind.
Rain soaked lawn,
pollen being blasted off the leaves,
oil from the roads.
The morning mixture fills my nostrils,
cross-country memories pop into my head.

As I step away from the porch and head down the street,
the rain comes harder, bouncing off the asphalt and
resonating as if thunderous applause, sending me wet and
happy into my morning run, a smile upon my face.

**"How is it that running in the dark
brings me such clarity?"
#CrystalClearIdeas**
-BJSiddons

Running with Patience

After years, even decades, of running, opportunities are presented that help us discover training programs that work best for our age. Body tweaks and squeaks are matched only by the adjustments we must make to our workouts.

Early in our running, especially when we were young, a wide margin of error existed for our overzealous training and racing. Some were lucky enough to rage through and continue with no ills, however most of us had to micro-manage the highs and lows of good days and bad as we battled to prevent season ending injuries.

I've been working hard to manage my running as I train in earnest for a Boston Qualifier (BQ), a marathon finish time required by the Boston Athletic Association (BAA) that runners need, based on age, to enter and run the Boston Marathon. Training is a joy for me, especially over the past few years with my running group. Heading out for a group run or a solo adventure, five or six days a week, feeling like I am ready and able for the task, is incredibly energizing.

Injuries and setbacks of the past live in my ink pen, and as I sketch out my training schedules I adjust plans to maintain a pain-free cycle, becoming ever more creative with workouts to stay healthy and keep improving. Otherwise, I'm just writing a prescription with liquid courage for knee pain, bursitis, a hip pointer, etc, etc, etc.

Reaching goals in running is a blast. Being patient enough to wait for them is hard. As I reset for the rest of this year, I know it's a blessing just to be out there. I want to push myself, dig deep and see if I can reach the goals I have set, but I must keep things in perspective. Much as I would love to bust-it-out on runs three or four days a week, I know two effort days and a long run are my keys to success. I'll keep testing, even after all these years, but as a seasoned runner I know it's a fine line between pushing yourself through the wall and hitting your head against it.

Mile in My Shoes – More than Running

I had only shown up once before, and that day it was a small group of 10 to 12. As runners, we show up early. The residents hadn't arrived. Very small talk between the three of us as we waited for the leader of the run to arrive. Today, the group training run for Mile in My Shoes was different. There must have been 30 people in the small courtyard outside the coffee shop as I drove by to find a place to park, and I was 15 minutes early.

Mile in My Shoes is a well-organized, volunteer organization aimed at helping homeless, and those in transition, gain the benefits running can bring into a person's life. Runners are asked to join the group runs and team up with a resident for the training sessions. Mile in My Shoes, was launched in May of 2014 by Mishka Vertin and Michael Jurasits, in partnership with Catholic Charities Higher Ground of Minneapolis. Since Mile in My Shoes founding, 400 members have laced up new shoes and run their very first mile.

About a year ago I drove to St Paul and ran with a resident named Peter. We just sort of fell into the same pace and ran the eight miles together. Mile in My Shoes had helped him train for and finish the Twin Cities Marathon the previous fall, something Peter was very proud of. "I'm a marathoner," he told me.

I could hear the passion in his voice and knew the program was doing exactly what the organizers had envisioned. It was more about life than running, and Peter was feeling positive about both.

Peter and I recognized each other today and we said hello before the run. As the pacing groups were being set, I ended up with the 12-mile group shooting for a 9:30 average pace. It was 7:00 am and the air temp was already nearly 70', with humidity nearly as high. There was also a dusky feel from smoke filtering in from California brush and forest fires. It was going to be a sweaty run.

The runners snaked along an asphalt path high above the west bank of the Mississippi River. There must have been 50 runners in total, a fantastic testament to the program. About a quarter mile in, as the leaders did their final pairings, I was asked to join up with Gabe, a guy that was planning to run eight miles. After I double checked the route, Gabe and I began to run side by side and settled in for the run.

Conversation was light. The usual back and forth about pacing, recent training runs and, of course, the weather. When strangers meet for a run there's a pretty big gap of common ground, other than running. Gabe's recent training had been mainly upper body weight workouts and swimming, so his current running fitness was not where it had been.

Even so, he held a steady pace and we didn't stop until the first water fountain, about a mile and a half into the run. Other runners from the group had also gathered there, including Peter. We took a drink and headed back out on the path. Now on the east side bluffs, we caught a glimpse of some rowers on the smooth as glass Mississippi. We are lucky to have so many scenic options to run, bike and walk in the greater Twin Cities area.

We dialed back the pace as we began to head up a few hills on the course. This is a part of the Medtronic Twin Cities Marathon where many runners struggle, and includes the mile where Brooks offers a free pair of shoes if you can run it faster than your average pace. Smart promo.

A bit later we hit another water fountain and caught up with a few others in the group. At this point Gabe was really feeling the heat and humidity. We decided to head back to the start/finish area and cut the run back to five miles, although it would still feel like eight. It was a good move for Gabe. He was able to finish with a steady pace and said he would try and get out more frequently, even if it was just a short two or three-mile run, to build his base. I thanked him for the run and headed back out for another five miles.

I ran along the same route, so, lucky me, I was able to run the hill portion again. Which is fine, as I will be racing the Twin Cities 10 Mile in October. It follows the last six miles of the marathon, so I figured 2.5 miles out, turn around and head back for five. A total of 10 for the day.

As I ran my five miles, I thought about all the hours people put in to keep groups like this going, and all the events we, as runners, participate in. I realized how little I do to give back. There is room in my life for more volunteer hours and I need to set a schedule like I do for my training. It felt good to join the group today and offer some words of encouragement to a fellow runner. Knowing how hard Gabe worked during our run together was inspiring to me and helped me work harder on my five-mile portion.

The main draw for me to show up at a Mile in My Shoes workout is empathy. I've had some hard times, and it sucks. Running has, for over 40 years, been an outlet for me to vent frustrations and flush out some demons. It has also allowed me to meditate while being physically active and work through life issues.

Running, more than anything, has been the conduit through which; anger turns into calm, anxiety turns into confidence, challenges turn into victories, disappointment turns into understanding, loss turns into growth.

Running isn't the answer for everyone. But for me, and for those in the Mile in My Shoes program, it's a road toward a better life, one mile at a time.

www.mileinmyshoes.mn

Faith Along the Way

Three weeks from this Saturday will by my third marathon in one year. Last October was the Medtronic Twin Cities Marathon in Minneapolis/St. Paul, this past June was Grandma's Marathon in Duluth, and now Jeanette and I will be running the Whistle Stop Marathon in Ashland, Wisconsin. For me, that's more marathons than I've run in the previous ten years, combined. I've always run, it's just that I have not geared up for long runs and races. In fact, I hardly race at all.

Recently, I finished a training run with my main running partner, Dave, and we began to talk about how we've both been re-energized to run over the past month. After a tough day at Grandma's (conditions were hot and humid and we missed our goal by just over four minutes) there was the usual post-race let down, a bit more in this case because of our slower times. After six weeks or so our bodies were recovered and spirits were high. Our runs started to show we were getting in decent shape and the drive to run faster was coming around.

Runners don't get many 'atta boys or 'atta girls during the many weeks and months of training. We run and train because we love it, because it brings focus and order to our life. A good run can really make your day, or week. Plus, we don't need to compare our pace with anyone else. My pace may be a slow jog for Fast Freddie, or too quick for Summer Slowguy. But for all of us, a good run shows us our progress. A solid workout rekindles our desire to reach our goals and gives us hope that the early morning workouts and long weekend runs are paying off. It's so fun to experience.

The power of running is not in the race times we reach as individuals, it's how we interact with others as we strive to those results. Enjoy your training, it's 99% of what we do.

More than a Runner

Soft workout tee, faded blue,
Well used, soaked with sweat.
My favorite, worn so often,
Becomes tattered too soon.

Morning runs before dawn,
Through neighborhoods and parks.
Muscles, mind and spirit
Renewed with the rising sun.

Filled with a gratefulness for the
Ways in which running grants
Peace, Joy, Health, Friendship,
Serenity, Challenges, Adventure.

A relationship with running is
Earned with each stride,
Yet not guaranteed to survive unless
Nurtured with compromise, patience and respect.

We honor the craft of training,
It's myriad aspects of improvement go
Far beyond longer distances, and faster times.
We dig deep in hope of uncovering our true self.

Once found, we relish the potential of
The whole person we can become;
After the workout, after the race, after our
Superhero shoes are removed.

Celebrating 60: Took longer than expected.

I've been looking forward to spring 2018 for a couple of years now. Turning age 60 was at the forefront of my thoughts and included things like feeling lucky to be healthy, spending time with my wonderful wife and seeing my children continue along the path of life via schooling, marriage and bringing our first grandchild into the world. Reflections on the past have been bouncing around inside of my head, but the push to keep reaching for new goals, adventures and lessons in life is as strong as it's ever been.

Last fall, Jeanette and I decided to sign up for this year's Boston Marathon, which is currently number one on the focus chart. Although we had both qualified with times over ten minutes faster than our respective age groups required, life was speeding by and we nearly let the opportunity pass. There will come another time that fits better with everyone's schedule, we told ourselves. Let's wait until the boys are out of school and our grandson is older, then everyone can go, we figured. It wasn't long until our friends and family let us know we had to sign up for 2018, with many good reasons to do so. The top two reasons were, one, "Because you never know what life will bring.", followed closely by, "When will we both qualify again in the same year?" We signed up and we are incredibly thankful for their encouragement.

As a lifelong runner midway through my fourth decade of running, I can detect when my training is going well. The last couple of years I have had, for me, decent results in the few races I've done. Looking ahead at entering a new age group, I've been motivated to line up my training to see what I can accomplish over the next few years.

It's been well over 30 years since my marathon PR of 2:59.48, but I feel ready to try and see if I can dip under 3:38 at age 60. I'd call that a successful season and something I should go after before it's too late. Previous to Jeanette and I signing up for Boston, I and a friend had signed up to race the Fargo Marathon in May, just five weeks after Boston. I've been double-motivated this winter to be prepared for these two events, something that, while exciting, does come with a front seat on the roller-coaster of long-distance running.

Training in Minnesota for an April marathon does have its drawbacks. Prime running weather it is not, so we've put in many miles on treadmills at the local YMCA. With plenty of others around us also training for their own health and events, it really hasn't been too bad. In fact, the consistency of the 'mill has brought us into spring in decent shape. Coupled with a few long outdoor runs, things are looking good for April 16. Boston will be a celebration run for J'net and me. We're looking forward to enjoying our run together and soaking in all that race day has to offer for first timers, as well as spending time in the greater Boston area a few days ahead of and after the marathon to visit some historic sites.

One thing I've learned over the past few years is that to gain a PR (in my case an Age Group PR) you need to remember it can also stand for Patience and Recovery. This struck again the day before my birthday. I had run my first 20-mile training run of the season on a Saturday and it had gone well. The following Tuesday progressive run was paced a bit easier for some extra recovery. After a light day on Wednesday, my Thursday morning pace run was proceeding just fine. Six and a half miles into the run I felt a slight twinge on the instep of my right foot. Okay, I thought, just a passing tweak. A few strides later I had to step off the treadmill belt and massage my foot. I had felt a much deeper twinge. Foot massaged and stretched, I was back on the treadmill. It took only a few strides to realize my run was over.

This was a brand-new pain, and a sharp one at that. I let J'net, who was running on a treadmill next to me, know that I was done with my run and I'd meet her downstairs. Heading to the locker room I wasn't worried about running the next day, I was worried about finishing Boston in six weeks!

Injuries are a part of long-distance running, and as we age they pop up much more frequently. It's difficult to re-train yourself in the battle against injuries. We are challenged with knowing when to hold off from running more often even when you feel good, and when to lay back when you really want to push harder. It's even tougher still when you feel you've taken the precautions to stay healthy and a new malady shows up, as was the case with my right foot. I didn't hesitate on treatment; Advil, ice, massage and stretching. Oh, and no running for three days. Not the way I wanted my first running weekend at age 60 to play out, but it was a hard luck reminder of how quickly things can change.

Having time to try and figure out what happened, I surmised that since my right foot strikes the ground at a straighter angle than my left, it was taking slightly more of a hit on the treadmill. Each time my right foot came forward it caught just a bit more of the resistance the belt feeds back in its reverse motion, especially during faster workouts, and eventually my foot gave way to a breakdown. At least that's what I'm going with for now.

Forced rest isn't always a bad thing, "You won't lose any fitness" was the mantra from J'net and my running friends. I agreed and let the weekend pass with a bit more birthday celebrating and eating than I had planned, but it was all good. Sixty only comes around once in a lifetime.

By Monday evening things were going much better. My treatment had paid off and I was heading out the door with J'net for an easy five-miler to test out my foot. I did change the lacing on my running shoes. I was not using the upper eyelets in hopes it would ease the pressure on my instep.

Throughout the run my foot felt fine, even as we sidestepped patches of snow and ice on the asphalt path through our local park. By the time we returned I was very pleased that my foot had totally ignored the effort. No pain, no stiffness.

My fears of not running Boston were put to rest. Of course, I was not taking the quick recovery for granted. The previous fall I pulled a calf muscle and was out from running for six weeks, with another six weeks to get back to a basic fitness level. Three days off was no big deal, and the next evening I headed out for an effort run. Usually on Tuesdays I do a progressive workout, starting with a warm-up mile, then dropping 15 to 30 seconds each mile or two. On the treadmill I had worked up to doing the last five of eight miles at 7:30 pace. This had taken about five weeks to accomplish. During those weeks I had substituted one of the progressive runs for a workout of 3 x 2 miles at 7:14 pace for something different. This would be my first outdoor effort run of the season, and my first age 60 effort.

Sometimes you know right away how the run may go. Taking shorter strides as I began, I felt better than I had figured I would. It had taken me a while to get out the door to run after arriving home from work. I delayed myself a couple times and almost didn't get out. Down the block I went, gauging my effort from the start. A couple turns and I had a nice flat stretch ahead of me to get into rhythm. It was working. After two miles I knew I had started out well, even though I don't look at my GPS watch on these runs, I told myself, "It's good to run fatigued." About the third mile in my system was, as I like to say, fully operational; lungs full, blood flowing, mind locked in on the goal.

Just before the first of three moderate up-hills started, I was debating between a six- or eight-mile distance for the workout. Six seemed not long enough, even at the effort I was putting out, but eight, after the foot thing, seemed like it would be pushing it. I settled on seven.

Heading up the first incline I thought of my Boston Buddies and the many hill repeats they had worked through. Motivation from thinking of them hitting their hills got me through the roughly two miles that included three inclines and declines. After that section the out and back course was mostly flat with just a few subtle rises through neighborhoods. The last stretch was the same section that got me rolling and was a blast to head back home along. "This is what running is." I said to myself. Body working, mind on task, goal being met with a solid effort. It was fun!

Nearing the last turn into my neighborhood I kept steady. No kick, just keeping the effort going, knowing I had worked harder the last two miles. When the mile seven beep sounded on my watch, I intentionally kept going for a few more strides, knowing I could have run longer. I hit the stop button and began my cool down jog.

I play the pace game many runners do before they look at their watch. You begin to guess how the run felt, and what the pace will end up being, secretly hoping for a 'faster than it felt' time. I did feel the run had gone well, and I figured low 7:40's, maybe high to mid 7:30's. I looked at the total time, did some quick math (not my strong suit) and figured, "Oh, 7:40's." Kinda bummed, but then remembered, "Hey, I ran seven miles, not six." Final overall pace was 7:27, five seconds faster than my best mid-distance workout last year. I was much happier, especially since I finished the last two going 7:20 and 7:10, feeling good.

As disappointed as I had been a mere five days earlier as I walked away from the treadmill with a sore foot, the turnaround was worth it. I was humbled with an injury, then humbled again with a workout that told me things are going to be okay. Stick with the plan, absorb the shocks of the roller-coaster with calm, and then get right back at it once it's go time. Turning 60 and being midway through my fourth decade of running, it's great to get as excited about running as I did in my youth. I'm still learning, and it's awesome.

**"Running is measured by more than mileage and time.
Months, years and decades are the true markers
of the long-distance runner."
#LifeIsAnUltraMarathon**
-BJSiddons

Little Jar of Matchsticks

So often it's the little gains that make a difference in the big picture. Unassuming moments, hidden from view and hardly mentioned. Like the easy 4 mile run I almost didn't go on, and would have missed seeing the pair of fawns, under the watchful eyes of their nearby mother doe, in the park.

It would be worth collecting something small, say, wooden matchsticks, for each Little Wonder I experience while on a run. And a collection for the big moments, too. Dropped into Mason jars, gathering a collection of memories as the year runs by.

Today I would have added a matchstick to the Little Wonders jar after a morning run with J'net and Dave. Actually, two match sticks. First, one for the pleasure of being able to run with J'net and my main training partner. We mix our training speeds and distances depending on the day. It's a cooperative effort aimed at making sure everyone's able to get in a workout and enjoy each other's company. My second matchstick would be dropped into the jar as a thank you to Dave for pulling me along to a faster pace today. It's been about two months since I ran the Lake Wobegon Marathon, as a workout, and I've been in a bit of a training slump. We've done a couple of interval sessions, but I was just feeling off. So today we warmed up running a few miles with J'net, then Dave and I picked it up for two miles...and it felt great. Running faster is fun, especially when the effort seems easier than the Garmin shows. We cruised for another two miles through Bunker Park then stopped when our friend, Bryan, came running the opposite direction. A short conversation ensued and suddenly the three of us were headed back home at a nice clip. I just love the feeling of a steady pace with friends, especially on a path lined with pines and prairie grass escorting us to the finish.

With runs like these I'm sure by the end of the year my Mason jar of Little Wonders would be filled with matchsticks. Come January, sitting by a fire, I can see myself lighting each matchstick as I try to recall as many memories from throughout the year as I could remember, smiling about each one.

Even though these Little Wonders come and go daily without much fanfare, like an easy four-mile run, they make a bigger impact on my life than I might have allowed myself to realize. Not anymore. From now on I'll savor the little things even more, comfortable in the knowledge that I'll have a jar full of fire to light the way into a new year.

**"I don't run every day, but every day I run,
well, it's awesome!"
#LikeMeSomeJogging**
-BJSiddons

Family Runs During the Holidays

During the holiday season, the rush of activity can make it tough to fit in a workout, much less get out extra early for a long run. On the plus side, we have more opportunity to run with family and friends, or those visiting from out of town, which in my case is our son, Spencer, home from college on winter break. Thanks to texting and Facebook, it's easier to schedule a group outing.

Holiday runs with family and friends are always enjoyable. Running at a pace everyone can manage, conversing on topics that are upbeat and not centered on training or racing, these runs remind us how energizing it is to make time for true social runs at a time of year when we are trying to both repair our bodies and recharge our spirits.

One year I had the good fortune of being able to have a Thanksgiving family vacation. We flew out to California and I was able to have a couple of runs with my brother, Al, and then race a half-marathon with my brother-in-law Gary and my sister-in-law Carolyn. The week after the race, the nine of us that are runners ran easy in the hills near Carolyn's home, heading out to traverse the dirt trails on cool, crisp mornings. Being with family during the holidays is a blessing and having family to run with and enjoy the outdoors is a double bonus. Not everyone needs to run, of course, just taking time to be active outdoors together does wonders for our physical and mental fitness levels.

Make time to enjoy running or walking with your non-regulars over the holidays. Send a text or make a call to set up a run and then a stop for coffee after. You'll be glad you shared the time together.

Until Next Time

Missing you right now.
The fix, the rush, the joy.
It's a slow start each time,
Easing into the groove.
Hurry won't quench me, I need
A well-planned session.

When you're taken from me,
Not available, or I'm not able,
I struggle.
I may wander, but
I am never fulfilled.
Other options may tease me, but
Only you can satisfy.

I'm forever at your mercy,
Until I'm whole again.
Resisting the urge that
Pulls at me each morning.
Temptation so strong, yet,
I won't take a step outside.
Hungry to redeem
The longing, and
The angst, while I
Fight to recall
The ballast that
Keeps my life on keel.

I'm lucky, I know.
The heartbreak could have
Dealt me a harder blow.
In truth, it was,
A fortunate fall, with;
Helping hands to aid me.
Thoughtful words to console me.
Tender mercies to heal me.

As I make my way,
Through these first fuzzy days,
While slightly askew, I'm
Stronger for the experience.
Yet it's still no consolation.
I'd rather be out there,
Going for it, getting after it.
Stoking passion into a
Controlled effort until I'm
Flush with a refreshing feeling of
Pleasant exhaustion.

The waiting, I'll learn to deal.
The unknown, that may be scary.
From the peak of fitness, to the
Crush of plans gone totally awry.
Not sure re-entry, will, for me,
Have the outcome I so
Desperately yearn for.

And yet, I know,
One day,
We'll be back together.
Me, and
The roads,
The trails,
The ovals.
The warm-ups and cool downs,
The hill repeats and intervals.
Long runs and tempos,
Recovery pace and rest days.
Sympatico.

In stride,
In motion, as if...
Nothing,
Ever,
Happened.

Ups and Downs of the Season

At my age, running is measured in decades, so I've got that going for me.

Setbacks that last a few weeks, or a couple of months, don't cripple a competitive season for me as it would a younger runner. Seasons are measured in years, not weeks or months. The cumulative effect of training from year to year is my friend, and I've embraced the fact that life throws curves, sliders and knuckle balls just when you're feeling the groove and crushing down-the-pipe fastballs.

It's not that things get in the way of running, there's always time for a few miles each day. My heart is comforted knowing that the ups and downs of training are as natural as the hills we encounter on our favorite trail run.

Last year was a great example. It started with a nice base that culminated with a 15k trail race in early spring. Late spring brought on tempo, speedwork and endurance runs, geared toward racing some shorter distances. Al finally got me into a couple of track races, something I hadn't done in over 40 years, and I loved it. He and I ran a 5k on the track and it's something I'll remember forever. I finished the summer season with a hard 5k road race and figured I'd sneak in a couple more road races to end the calendar year.

Standing at the plate, ready to swing; sinker, slider, curve...I strike out and find myself walking back to the dugout. Or, in my case, the freezer for an ice pack.

The year of a more intensive training schedule finally caught up with me in early fall, before I could race again, and I realized it was time to ease up for the year. After a couple of months trying to run through the nagging hamstring and leg stress, I finally took three weeks completely off from running. It was tough to do, but my long-term goals favored a complete recovery, even if it took months.

There's nothing worse than coming back from an injury too soon and having to start recovery all over again. It was worth the time, and although a mental struggle, I was finally able to leave the ice pack and extra stretching behind.

The New Year was upon us and a mild winter ensued. The opportunity to get in more training runs had been ample, allowing miles and sessions to gain momentum. We were spoiled, and over the next few weeks that feeling of turning fastballs into line-drives returned. The Yin was great, but the Yang streaked a solid hit into the gap.

The ups and downs continue, and now it's cold season, sending me back into the dugout for a week. Not sleeping much, congested, coughing, you know the drill. Sure, it's a first world problem that pales in comparison to the daily struggles of many, so I'm fine with a few days off. Like I said, I'm looking long term. Not that I have lots of decades left, but some time off is a small price to pay for an activity that enhances my life with so many positive aspects.

I'll be back at the plate soon, just in time for spring training.

**"Don't discount an easy four-mile run,
small gains add up to big goals."
#ItsTheLittleStuffInBetween**
-BJSiddons

Benchmarks

We have a 2x4 in our garage that's part of the support system for a few plywood shelves that are holding way too much stuff. Should we ever move, I'll have to replace it, even though it's irreplaceable. Over the years we have been marking this big 'ol yardstick with height checks of our kids, some neighbor kids, a couple of their friends and a relative or two. It's structurally important for our storage, but it's emotionally priceless as a reminder of each person's journey through the years.

Benchmarks are great tools and come in a multitude of options. For my running, I love to measure up against my previous seasons during training, as our group did last Sunday for our first long-run test. We wanted to see how our marathon training was preparing us for race day, and we all scored higher than we had planned. It was a good day to race, a fun atmosphere and plenty of positive vibes. No worries about the faster runners that finished ahead of us, no remarks about the slower runners doing their own thing.

Every runner has their own race to run, their own goals to strive for. While the individuality of running allows us to enjoy some anonymity as we reach for our own PR's, a race day collection of runners crossing the finish line, a virtual 2x4 of race times, creates a lifelong memory that is irreplaceable.

Inside the Run

There's a slice of my day,
Cut just the way I like it.
Early morning hours,
quiet and crisp,
The rising sun generously
Spreading light and warmth
Upon the ground I tread.

Most days I'm alone as I run,
Sounds of suburbia of no concern to me.
I enter the park and the town fades away,
Its noise, its people, its reality,
Dropped from my thoughts along the path,
Imaginary guides I'll reload upon my return.

A mile into the run
I am nearly transformed.
Heartbeat now steady,
Breathing now regular.
As I hit the days pace
My body feels in tune.
My clarity of purpose,
Crystalized.

Wrapped in a shield of
Sweat and effort, this
Cocoon of running allows
Complete serenity.
I become one
With the surroundings,
Integrating my physical and
Mental status with each stride.

Minutes or hours,
Easy or hard,
Inside the run,
I find my place of solace.
Energy returned.
Soul cleansed.
Spirit rejuvenated.
Confidence elevated.

My time within the run is
A place like no other.
Fully aware of each motion I make, and yet
The rest of the world is beyond my shroud.
There, but not there.
Kept at bay by each breath I take
Until I choose to uncloak myself from the run.
Reborn,
Ready to embrace a new day.

Miles in the Bank

Friday night, party night...not! I'm in-training for Grandma's Marathon in Duluth, MN, and tomorrow morning it's a 5:30am wake-up call to run with Dave at 6:30am. After a very busy week of work and family life, it's an early dinner and then plenty of sleep.

Tomorrow marks 19 weeks out from race day, so this coming week is the last week of 'casual' training. Then the 18-week program begins. I'm really looking forward to this session, partly due to a mild winter that helped me maintain a decent fitness level without having to battle too tough of a winter. Even though we have February and March ahead, all indicators point to a very early spring.

Seasoned marathoners know the best way of getting to the start line of a race is by training smart. We have learned to embrace the season and be patient with our progress during the three to four months that lead up to race day. Keeping a positive attitude on the rough days and being thankful for the good days go a long way in staying motivated. Newbies seem to focus more on the anxiety of race day, and don't really understand the essence of what the training season is all about.

In training terms, "miles in the bank" is an excellent investment. The only way you can survive a decent marathon pace is to be able to "make a withdraw" on race day from your miles invested. If you haven't put in the time on your legs or the quality miles in your sessions, you will come up short on race day.

It takes a race or two before most people discover the benefits of investing in race day. If you have ever tried to explain a race, of any distance, to someone that is training for their first one, you know their understanding really doesn't sink in until after they have competed a couple of said event. That's ok, we don't know what we don't know.

Once we do begin to discover the secrets that work for us, it's great to unlock our passion with a better course that will then lead to more satisfying results. The journey is always sweeter when filled with self-discovery, and no matter the final outcome, if I've been able to make sound investments into my fitness level throughout the training season, I'll gladly take whatever dividends race day provides.

"There are few limits to our running...if we have honestly maximized that with which we are blessed."
#HaveIGivenItAllThatICan
-BJSiddons

Goals Versus Attainables

I was captivated by an interview with Sir James Dyson, inventor of the modern-day vacuum, on NPR this past weekend. My attention spiked when the subject of running came up. Sir James ran distance races, which came in handy when the interviewer asked him how he got through the tough times early on in the engineering and product development process of his breakthrough vacuum design. Deep in debt, no orders, no production, no light at the end of the tunnel. Dyson said, "I did long-distance running at school. And you only succeed by doing a huge amount of training and then having great stamina. Understanding that other people are also feeling tired, so when you feel tired, you should accelerate. That's when you start winning."

This really clicked for me, as I have been working on stepping up the mental side of my training and racing. How, I wonder, can we uncover our ability to break through when we feel broken, unless we attempt the un-obtainable?

Should our goals ever be reachable?

I began thinking, have I been taking the easy path and setting Attain-ables? Hitting most of my running goals the past two years, albeit with plenty of hard work and successful race day executions, looking over the past few months it appears I've been holding myself back from even greater personal success.

I don't need to drop from pure exhaustion at the end of a workout, that's for certain, nor do I need to puke at the end of every race. And, as much as I love Pre's quotes, I won't be bleeding to beat the person nearest me.

The process I need to break through won't be an easy task, and it will come with a couple of healthy doses of race-day pain and agony, and that's okay. The built-in limits my brain turns on as I head out for a workout or plan a race have been molded over decades of running. I'm sure I'll need many trials to crack open the protective shell I've been running within.

I'm not planning on going out at a crazy pace for key training days or races, but I will need to unlock the self-protection mode if I am ever going to reach new limits, if I am ever going to beat the inner self when I tire and, as Sir James Dyson said, "accelerate". Sure, I'll end up with some crash-and-burn efforts but, I will view them as lessons, not failures.

As I age, I yearn for just two things of my running: a run done well when called for and the ability to break through new barriers. I won't be as fast as I once was, but I do expect to maximize what I have, while I can, and that will be my breakthrough.

"Allow yourself the opportunity to succeed,
you've earned it."
#TrainingPaysOff
-BJSiddons

An Unexpected Running Experience: The 2017 Lake Wobegon Trail Marathon

Having just finished Matt Fitzgerald's book, "How Bad Do You Want It? The Psychology of Mind Over Muscle," I was intrigued by the mental toughness tools used by the world-class athletes Fitzgerald cited, specifically race day focus, as aids to improve my own running performances. Looking back at my BQ in the fall of 2012, for a spot at the Boston Marathon in 2014, and then missing the revised cut by six seconds, I wondered if my focus had been better, wouldn't I have run at least seven seconds faster?

While the stories Fitzgerald recounted were truly inspirational, I realized my quest for sharper mental performances might best be served through the experiences of runners fighting battles for improvements much less daunting than national championships or major marathon titles. Little did I know that within a week of finishing the last chapter, I'd be a participatory eyewitness to dozens of said runners, during the Lake Wobegon Trail Marathon, doing their best to show me the way. It would turn out to be my slowest marathon ever, and yet, running alongside my good friend and training partner, Stan, it would be one of the most incredibly positive events in my 40 plus years of running experiences.

Getting to the starting line of this marathon began innocently enough. Over the years, well decades, of my training, I've learned that to fend off injury setbacks it's extremely important to be patient with our recovery days, not be a patient in recovery. Stan, too, is well-aware of the need to stay healthy. His recent marathon training programs have left him over trained with forced time off, usually at the crucial one month from race day timeline, resulting in slower than normal finishing times.

In January, while discussing his most recent marathon crashes, we started talking about getting him back to his previous sub 3:55 finishing times for an attempt at a 60-64 age group BQ in a couple of years. As an alternative to his recent training regimes, he agreed to follow a program I would design and guide him through for his next marathon, and then build on the results for his BQ race. Stan, or Laser as we call him due to his laser-like focus, was unsure at first. After a few runs and some table talks about how the training would work, he was all in. We'd take a low-key approach; he'd be slightly undertrained, but 100% healthy with no injury down time. Our race-day time goal of a modest 3:59.59, with a secondary goal of 3:54.59, both well within his capabilities, were the foundation for our training paces. The Lake Wobegon Trail Marathon, where he had run his PR of 3:46 in 2013, was the easy choice for our race day effort on May 13, 2017.

Local, rural marathons are a meandering tour through wonderfully quaint places, and Lake Wobegon is right there with the best of them. From the early morning, friendly faces that direct you to catch a bus to the starting line of this point to point course, to each of the volunteers along the way, you are surrounded by great people all morning long.

The marathon begins on the Holdingford High School track and follows a single road for one and a half miles to the Lake Wobegon Trail, where you then run along a paved-over train line to the finish. Leafed out trees shade much of the first-half of the course, which then opens up to running through a few small towns, along lakes and in clear view of gentle rolling acreage. The scenic course is very flat, with the exception of one small grade at mile ten, that even I don't mind.

Aid stations are handled by helpful locals making time to support the event. With a limit of 450 runners, the participant mix is that of a few runners looking for fast times, others that have heard about what a fantastic event Wobegon is, plenty of return finishers and of course those that are on their maiden marathon trek.

Marathon training is a love affair with the running life. We run with tunnel vision, looking the only direction we can, forward, to the light of race day. The blinders we proudly wear keep us safe from distractions that would otherwise impede the progress we desire, that of inching closer to the escape hatch known as the starting line. We plan, we adjust, we sacrifice, we prepare. We chart our course like a salty ship captain returning to a cluster of islands known for coral reefs, rough seas and unexpected swells. When we break through the trials of training and into the light, race day can be its own master.

The best laid plans may need to be discarded when the winds of marathon day rise. Some days we must go where the breeze takes us, for to battle the wind is akin to fighting an invisible enemy you'd never see attack or regroup. You will be left flailing until you fall, overcome by your inability to admit this particular day is not for winning, but for surviving. And sometimes, if you are lucky, I mean really lucky, you are presented with a life changing experience.

Committing to a new training program is a tough challenge, and Laser did a fantastic job of staying with mine. He would sometimes admit to feeling short on the long run tally, as our longest ended up being 18 versus his normal dose of a few 20-milers. On the interval score, Laser had done an amazing job. In addition to some half-mile and mile repeats, he came through with flying colors on one of our most challenging workout sessions, 2 times 2 miles.

We'd warm-up with an easy mile and a half, then run two miles at tempo pace, take a three-minute easy jog interval, then run another two miles at tempo, followed by an easy mile cool down. Laser did this twice on the treadmill before the weather warmed up and we began training outdoors.

After a ten-mile race in April, which we did not peak for, we began to back off of the intervals and work on endurance. A couple of weeks into this part of the training, Laser felt that his legs were really getting under him and his trust in the program grew. The tenuous walk along the rail of fitness is a tough balancing act and we were now on our third and most important section of the training program. Laser began to leave the muscle ache of intervals behind and find his endurance, and now I was becoming more confident that we just may have his training program dialed in for race day success.

Early on in training, marathon race day looms on the horizon like a hillside just beyond reach. We move toward it for weeks, when suddenly the marathon is now approaching us. The magnitude of the upcoming event hits hard. Our respect for the distance moves us to self-preservation mode and we begin our taper. With weekly mileage in the 45-55 mile range, we taper only moderately for two weeks. The pace is easier, and we begin to allow the feeling of being race-ready to envelop us like a comfortable hoody and pair of sweat-pants after a tough workout. Laser and I had this final part of training set and made only a few minor tweaks, due to his busy schedule of moving his college age kids back home from school. Not the best thing to be doing during taper, but he's done it before with no ill effects.

We did our pre-race planning at this point and addressed the elephant in the room; pacing for race day. Like so many marathoners, Laser has usually gone out trying to put a few minutes of cushion into the first-half of the race, knowing he would tire after 20. This would be my toughest challenge to him; slow the early miles down.

After much discussion we agreed, well, he acquiesced to my directive, to run the first six to seven miles at a few seconds slightly slower than race pace, (so as not to fade at the end and give back time in minutes) then run at pace until 20. After that we'd see what he had left for the final 10k. Besides, I reminded him, this was just a test event, a building block for later. He had nothing to lose and possibly a more fitting program to fine tune over the next couple of years. Again, he was all in and I inked the final copy of our race day plan as "Approved."

Late in the afternoon on Friday, the day before the race, Laser called. He was making sure I had left work early, so I had time to rest up before Saturday's race. He's such a good guy and taking time to check on me was cool. Trouble was, he sounded as if he had smoked a pack of cigarettes that morning. His 'allergy' that had kicked in a couple of days earlier had gotten much worse. Afterward I said to my wife, Jeanette, that I wouldn't be surprised if he woke up the next morning unable to speak...which sometimes isn't a terrible thing, as Laser can be a talker.

Race day morning I received a great wake-up text from Laser, "Let's run a marathon today!" Game on! I picked him up at 4:16 am and he sounded much better. He had a great attitude and during pre-race prep he showed few signs of any allergy problems. He had by-passed using over-the-counter meds for fear of dehydration or any other ill effects but had doubled up on his Nettie-pot use to clear his airways.

Once we had picked up our race number, we did the normal pre-race routines; pinned our numbers onto our shirts, felt excited/nervous and chatted with fellow runners. We made sure that plenty of Vaseline was lubed in all the right places, Lasers' water belt was filled, and my GU packs were slid into the pockets of my shorts. Check list complete.

The race began right on time at 7:00 am and we passed over the start line chip mat a few seconds later, taking a three-quarter lap on the high school track. As we moved along at 9:06 pace, Laser was almost giddy at how slow and comfortable the pace was. I was glad to see him rested and ready.

Marathon day is the celebration of a runners long-term investment of putting 'Miles in the bank,' to be ready for a major withdraw on race day. You can't fake a marathon, and there are penalties for not investing enough or making poor decisions, such as going out too fast. Investments, however, are never guaranteed, and at the last moment you may need to adjust your portfolio. Being fit for race day is one-part rest, one part eating right, and one part staying away from anything that will strain a muscle or get you sick. Some of these are in your control, some are not. And some, unfortunately, get through all your defenses to greet you on race day. Thus was the case for my star pupil, Laser, at this year's Lake Wobegon Trail Marathon.

It wasn't until we made it all the way to say, oh, mile two, that I began to feel something was awry with Laser. He had gotten quiet already, and there was something about his gait that seemed off. After six years of running alongside someone, it can be easy to notice even a slight change. I kept a close eye on my Garmin and decided to err on the side of an even slower than planned pace. If his allergy had been more than a reaction to pollen, be it a cold or virus, I didn't want him to use any more energy than needed as he warmed-up during the first half-dozen miles or so.

As we slid to 9:14 pace during the third and fourth miles, Laser made a couple of comments about "not feeling it yet" and getting just a bit grumpy. It was at this point that he admitted to not sleeping well the past few days, having no appetite and in general feeling run down. He wouldn't let himself think he was getting sick, it had to be allergies. Laser is one of the nicest guys I know, and one of the hardest on himself. He will gut out a training run on the toughest of days, be it 30 mile per hour snowstorms or 100' summer heat. Laser won't quit, and today, unbeknownst to us, would turn out to be his most arduous race-day test yet.

Local marathons with just a few hundred participants have a way of becoming a close-knit community of heartfelt supporters in a way larger events can't replicate. It's just more intimate, and you remember each other easier as you play leapfrog throughout the race. Early on it was Bladder Pack gal and guy, Vegas gal, Gatorade's in the shorts guy, and others. Around mile seven Laser and I noticed 'Headache guy'. He was walking on the side of the trail, looking as if a migraine was getting the best of him, but he was still moving. The other runners were a good distraction, but they couldn't hide the fact we had lost sight of the 3:57 pace group so soon. After testing the waters of Laser's condition for seven miles, I finally asked him to take the lead at mile eight. The next 12 miles were to be his section of the race and we had to make a move. Our plan was for him to find his groove and get us to the 20-mile point, where I would then take the rein and run us in. He lasted about a half-mile at nine-minute pace, slowed markedly, and began the internal fight against the mindset of defeat.

Our celebration of race day was not going as planned. The culmination of Laser's investments; the miles run, the early morning workouts, the change in eating habits, some tough intervals and the steady long runs were now just useless weights upon his shoulders. Where were the wings he had earned to carry him along to the finish?

At mile nine we began the conversation that was staring back at us every moment we looked at our Garmin's; What's our new plan?

Once a burden is laden upon you, while it's tough to carry, it can be even harder to accept the situation and let it fall away with your expectations. With Laser's hard-nosed desire to at least break 4 hours, and our sub goal of crossing under 3:55, admitting we wouldn't be close was becoming not only frustrating, but debilitating. The mind wanders to many places and is easily discouraged. You question everything about your training, your preparation and then complain about how unfair it is that you got sick just a couple of days ago. Yet amid all this we begin to see the signs of others struggling. We pass Headache guy again, this time around mile 12, not realizing he had passed us. Laser and I talk again about how badly that guy must be hurting, and it eases Laser's toiling slightly seeing someone else battling rough patches that seemed to come more frequently, and fiercely, as miles were added to our legs.

Continuing down the trail, we talk more seriously about letting go of our time goals. This reconciliation would take another few miles for Laser to agree that today would be a finish goal only, no time stamp to worry about. Just when I thought we were on the cusp of re-charting our way to the finish line; I realized my work was just beginning as our day came dangerously close to an abrupt end at the 14-mile point.

If you've ever experienced someone losing contact with their surroundings, especially during an athletic event, you know things can change in an instant. Tracking Laser, I realized he was showing signs of overall fatigue that went beyond being tired.

He was unknowingly weaving from side to side on the trail, his comments were sparse and not on point to the topic. His pace was very erratic. He easily overheats, and I began pouring water on him to cool him down.

"Let's run to that shade spot and then walk again," I suggested. He stopped the instant he hit the shade, and it was then I noticed his eyes wandering, his body swaying. "Laser, what day is it?" I asked. It caught him off guard and he faltered, both physically and emotionally. At just past the 14-mile point Laser was out of fuel, and mentally off course. He hesitated, then with stumbled verbiage found the words to give me the right answer, albeit with a raw, humbled emotion I had not seen from him before.

It was a tough couple of minutes down in that valley of doubt many runners have experienced. Walls crash down and yet there's always at least one path for a slow climb up. And that's what he did. Laser became characteristically focused and stated undeniably that he would make it to the finish line, walking the whole way if that's what it would take. He most certainly knew what day it was now.

Laser was back, but I let him know that I'd do all I could to get him off the course if he faltered as he had at mile 14. From that point on we walked when needed, he drank more fluids than he ever had, and downed extra gel (warm gel late in a race is not a runner's first choice, but he did it) to keep himself hydrated and nourished. It was at this point he finally let the finishing time burden slide off his shoulders, giving him a better outlook on the day. It was what it was. We were burning the chart and setting sail with the wind, not against it. We talked to more runners as we repeatedly passed and got passed. We made time at the aid stations to re-fill his bottles and get some of the snacks they offered later in the race.

We bantered with each other as if on a long training run. Our discussion topics ranged from running to kids, to work, to life goals. Heck, we had plenty of time and at this point everything was on the table to talk about. It's amazing how bare you can lay your soul on a long run with a good friend. We were cleansing our physical bodies mile after mile, and our emotional selves, topic after topic.

That's when Laser peeled back a whole lotta layers and laid out the core of his motivation. Growing up, when he had a tough task ahead or decided to go after a goal, he was told he'd never get it done, never accomplish anything, so don't even try. The classic, "You'll never amount to anything" rang in his ears and pierced his heart. He did his best to try and please a father that had little compassion, but it wasn't until years later that Laser would figure out his father was the lost soul. After that epiphany, Laser worked for what he wanted until he got it, and he has applied the same mentality to running. Be it a tough training day, hard intervals, or long training runs, he would prove his self-worth and accomplish his goals.

His words gave me insight to his overtraining and his disappointment when he didn't meet self-imposed expectations. I realized he still carries a few splinters from the cross he bore as a youth, but don't we all? If part of the ache in our hearts comes from a place so deep that, even to our physical detriment, we will do whatever it takes to finish, to succeed, to meet the goals that make us happy, how can we not keep running forward?

With ten miles to go, the comradery between runners at the five to six-hour pace grows stronger with each step. By this point you've seen each other a few times on the course, stopped at aid stations at the same time, and heard each other talk to running mates or supporters along the way.

For example, the two sisters. One was running, and the other would stop at different points and provide encouragement. It was great to see and gave us something to ask about when we ran alongside each other a couple of times. There was also the 70-74 guy. We must have passed each other a half-dozen times, exchanging words of support to each other. When we asked how many marathons he had run, he said "This is my first one...today." It gave us a good laugh.

With the wide variety of runners I was seeing, I began to realize this was my opportunity to take off my tunnel vision blinders and get a much broader view of what it takes to focus and fight through racing struggles. It's not about the pace, breaking through comes from a much deeper place. I saw five-hour finishers focused on the task at hand in a way that would equal any race winner. Men and women, young and old. Heads up, and heads being barely lifted. Bodies moving with little sway, and bodies bent at odd angles. Here I was with my running brother as he fought for every step just to run his worst time ever, on the same course he had set his PR, and these folks were doing all they could to set a PR, or at least have a good day. These were the regular runners I wanted to hear about.

There are certain points along the Lake Wobegon Marathon course that stand out. One of them is the 18-mile point, located in the small town of Avon. It's a landmark Laser enjoys for three reasons. First, it's 18 miles. Yay for that. Second, there are plenty of volunteers to help with filling water bottles and to hand out fluids. Third, it's a very easy point of access to the course for spectators, so there's always a nice cheering section about a half-mile long. It's a shot in the arm as you emerge from the isolation of the trail, get pumped up, and then head back out to the quiet and begin to concentrate on getting to 20.

Laser had rebounded and was running fairly steady as we came into Avon. We took full advantage of the aid station and the volunteers were awesome. I spotted a sponge, so I grabbed that to carry and occasionally cool Laser down, as the temp had snuck up to the low 70's with no cloud cover. Runners were showing the classic signs of heat fatigue, and with Laser's propensity to sweat on even the coldest of days, I would do all I could to rain water his way. The sponge, and for a while a small towel that I eventually handed off to another runner, would be in my possession to the finish.

Small victories are priceless in a marathon, and on this day, we'd take every one we could get. A couple of our best miles were from just before 19 to nearly 21. I had stopped to take a quick pee break, and as I came out, I tagged along with a guy we had seen running earlier with his wife. Laser had continued running during my break, and as is his habit he would keep up a slightly faster pace until I caught him.

It's a game he plays when he trains. Laser dislikes stopping on runs, so if someone needs a quick break for the bathroom, or, heaven forbid we stop at a traffic signal, he continues on. Even in his exhausted state, there he was, trucking down the trail, totally focused, looking like he was just out on a regular training run. The guy I was running with told me his wife had run ahead of him. He said they were looking for a race to run together and although he was more of a sprinter and she a distance runner, they comprised and choose the Lake Wobegon Marathon. Smart husband. Over the course of a half-mile or so we caught up to Laser. Sprint guy ran a few strides with us, more like shuffles, and then said he was going to try and catch up to his wife.

Laser was ready for another walk break, so we looked for some shade and walked toward a stretch just ahead. Grey Shirt guy, another of the leap-frog group, passed us again. He was doing well, keeping his own pace, sharing encouraging words with us. His wife, Concordia gal, would meet him at most of the aid stations and easy access spots along the course, typical of what we saw all day long. There's something about a marathon that brings out the best in spectators and fellow runners, especially during the later stages of the race. Seeing fresh faces and listening to the high spirits at the start, spectators that follow the race and continue their support are invaluable to a struggling runner. Spectators bear witness to the steady decline of both physical stature and emotional well-being that 26.2 miles heaps upon a participant. "Looking good" is great cheer for about eight miles, but after that it's a small fib for at least the next ten. After that we know they are lying, but we not only forgive them, we hang on to the belief that maybe we really don't look like wandering zombies searching for our next meal.

"It's like running from the five-mile bench, Laser," I said, referring to a landmark we use on one of our common routes. We had now passed the 21-mile marker and could picture the last few miles in a perspective he could envision.

"We're doing this!" I added.

"Oh, yeah, baby," Laser replied, and we started running again.

It was right around this point that we noticed Headache guy again. He was just in front of us, walking. As we came up to him, I asked him a simple question, "You want to run with us for a while?"

"Sure, I'll give it a try."

And that's how we met the guy that blew the blinders completely off our tunnel vision. Yes, we had gone full circle with the race up to that point, and Laser had allowed himself to be comfortable with just finishing the marathon. We had started with solid expectations, sunk deep into the ravine of regret, and then clawed and climbed up to the road again, heading to the finish. We still had over four miles to go, and anything could have happened to Laser in that span. Thankfully, Don happened.

It was hot, Laser had been giving all he could for miles, and we still had, at our pace, 40 to 50 minutes to go. I had us pegged for a 5:30 finish at one point, but Laser was making up time and we'd be under that, for sure. We had seen Don struggling at various points in the race, and, wanting to get an idea of his plans for the next few miles, I asked him, "So, it looks like you've been having a tough day. Are you having migraines or allergies?"

If that's all it had been.

That tunnel vision I had for racing my next marathon, that feeling of lust I get when trying to coax a few seconds from each mile I race, that disappointment I had after a good race that I wanted to be great? Yeah, I'll be tossing that out with the garbage after running with Don for those last few miles.

It's not that he's a saint, he's just a guy that wants to run and race like he used to, but after a couple of recent concussions he's had to let go of his burden of not being able to run after this race. And by this race, I mean his 60th marathon. At age 43. Oh, and he won this event in 2011 with a finishing time of 2:48.

"Actually, it's vertigo," Don said.

The next couple of miles, even at 12-minute pace, flew by as we talked about his background. Ten years ago, he was 230 pounds of inactivity until his brother got him to sign up for a 10k. Although more of a walk, the running bug had begun to infect Don. Slowly the training miles piled up, and then the racing began. Within two years of running, Don had a 3:31 marathon to his credit. Nice debut. The time drops continued until 2011, when he won the Lake Wobegon Trail Marathon. Along the way he dove into the running community by leading pace groups at different distances, including the marathon, which helped him add to his finish total without stressing his body too much. He volunteered at events and mentored other runners. Here was a guy getting it done and giving back in a big way.

"I've had a couple of serious concussions in the past few years. The vertigo has made it tough to run." Well, if you call headaches, dizziness, throwing up and falling down tough, yeah, I'd agree.

"Was that your wife helping you out at some of the aid stations?" I asked.

"No. I think she said she's a nurse and she saw I wasn't having such a good day and she just helped me out." Her name turned out the be Diane, and she is a nurse. (Don would meet her via Facebook after the race). While watching the race, Diane saw Don was not doing well. Her instincts kicked in and she made sure his aid station stops included plenty of fluids. They had never met, but, as Laser and I have done, she made a bond with Don that will last many years.

As Don related his running background, Laser and I looked at each other as the realization that things can always be worse had materialized right beside us. It was a wake-up call at just the right time for Laser. At somewhere between 23- and 24-miles Laser was running even lower on energy. His muscles were toast and only his sheer will was getting him from mile marker to mile marker. Hearing Don explain his challenges and then seeing him holding his head to stay on the course, and at one point falling to one knee, was more than what Laser needed to keep going. This wasn't a race anymore, it was escorting a fellow runner for the last few miles of what may be his last marathon, if not his last race.

Not far after the 24-mile marker we stopped for a walk break. It may seem crazy to most, but these breaks were very necessary. Two women runners offered us a cup of ice and a Nunn tablet, and Don gained some much-needed electrolytes. The generosity of fellow runners and spectators never wavered. We drank up and then began running once more.

My biggest challenge during the last few miles was to monitor my two co-runners. Laser was a little quieter and I knew he was in his zone, concentrating on getting to the finish. He was staying steady and only a couple of times did I need to pull him back on the trail, mainly when we were walking or getting water at an aid station. Same for Don, although he wobbled a bit more. If I had felt either one was in danger, I would have immediately asked a fellow runner or spectator for help, but these guys were keeping hydrated, answering questions and staying alert. I knew they would make the finish safely, but they'd be totally spent.

"Hey, guys, there's the 25- mile marker," I said. "Let's get there and then walk that shade part on the trail." We crept up to the marker and began a short walk in the shade. I could nearly read their minds, knowing they had only a mile point two to go, their heads were already seeing the finish line.

"Let's knock out the final mile without stopping," Don said. "We can do this."

"I'm in." Laser replied.

We ran silently for most of the last mile, three abreast. The pace was slow enough to be able to make the last mile, but at a slightly faster pace than what we had been running...a little pride was breaking through as we made our way down the straight, flat stretch toward our destination.

About three-quarters of a mile out you can pick up the red finish arch. A half-mile out you can see the balloons and hear the crowd. Our steps fell yet a bit faster, our heads held a little higher. Laser and Don had waged a fierce battle on this day, and they had full rights to run proudly in at 5:14.44.

Three steps over the finish line Don faded to the grass on the right and collapsed on all fours. Race staff, most of whom knew Don well, were there in a matter of seconds, and he was in the med-tent within a minute. I've never had vertigo but have seen people incapacitated from its effects.

Don had resigned himself to walking the last five miles, yet he gutted it out, like the champion he is, and ran in with us. About 20 minutes later I found out from the race director that Don's friends had taken him to the local hospital for an IV treatment to try and get the vertigo in line. Dang, that was one tough finish.

Laser had headed to the left side of the finish area, completely gassed from the race. His effort was clearly the most work I had ever seen him put out during a marathon. I told him how well he had done and what a great accomplishment today's race had been. As we talked over the next half-hour, I enjoyed hearing his description of how the race had turned into a very positive event. Laser's empathy for the other runners was bursting from his heart, especially for Don and the struggles he had overcome and would face in the future.

While not pleased with his own finishing time, Laser welcomed his place with the other back of the pack finishers that had dug deep and worked through the toughest of days not only physically, but had beat back the mental challenges they all faced. It was a tremendous boost to his confidence, and I was sure these feelings would grow and strengthen within him as we looked back on this day during future runs.

We sat and watched Grey Shirt guy finish, and 70-74 guy, too. Some of the other leap froggers that had finished before us came by to see how we were doing, and we asked how their day ended up. Between the pizza, cookies, Gatorade and treats, the conversations were leading Laser and I to a great conclusion.

This may have been one of our favorite marathons, ever. The multitude of mental battles, including Laser's and Don's, that had raged all around me during the event, right up to the final steps over the finish line, were just the scenarios I was looking for after reading Fitzgeralds' book.

I had been looking with tunnel vision for a sharper mental edge and was quietly presented with that gift, and more, by runners so full of heart it was impossible not to become a fan of each and every one of them.

Suddenly, I was taken aback by the latest announcement over the finish line speakers. It was something I had never heard at a marathon.

"Less than two minutes to get in. Come on, runner." As the race clock was counting down (or is it up?) to the six-hour cut-off time, the announcer let everyone know there was one runner coming down the trail that would be close to making the cut-off. But he'd have to earn it.

Hearing this, spectators began to fill in the finish chute area on both sides of the trail. Weary runners ambled over, the Girl Scouts from one of the last aid stations came with big smiles and cheers, as did others that had done volunteer work for the race that morning.

"Sixty seconds to go" came the update.

With the long straight-away of the marathon trail, you could see that Last guy was doing his best to make the time cut, laying down the fastest pace he could muster.

The crowd, although small, was doing their best 'Here comes a winner' cheer for a guy they had never met. No matter, it's what runners and friends of runners do. We support each other through thick and thin, on good days and not so good days.

As I was standing there, watching Last guy near the finish, (and eventually crossing the line with 48 seconds to spare) I catch sight of Laser. He had limped over to the finish area, pulled in by the drama unfolding before us, his hands clapping wildly and his voice cheering loudly, for a guy he didn't know, but now, more than ever, certainly understands. My running brother had the marathon experience of his life today, and I couldn't be prouder of him.

Race Day

The 'A' Goal for my race,
Laid bare for all to view.
Committed, not inhibited,
By the time I'd like to do.

It's a stretch, for sure,
Of that there is no doubt.
Yet I can't turn down this challenge,
To battle each step of the route.

Rising, some days at 4:30 a.m.,
I know I've put in the training.
Long runs, hard runs, fast runs,
It's all been good, I'm not complaining.

Physically in better shape than
I've been in many years.
This race now means so much to me,
Whatever the result, I'll be in tears.

The mental prep has started.
Focusing, planning, rehearsing how it goes.
I've got to execute this race perfectly,
So down the stretch I'll be on my toes.

Respecting the distance will keep me,
From going out too fast.
I've crashed and burned enough times,
I don't want to repeat that past.

Patience in the beginning.
Trust the plan while you hit stride.
Fortitude will keep you going.
Courage brings home the pride.

And when in the valley I find myself,
Struggling to keep my pace,
I'll recall those near and dear to me,
And their good wishes for this race.

The finish line, eventually,
Will come into my view.
Through blurry eyes, on tired legs,
I'll know just what to do.

Dig deep, dear runner, dig deep.
This journey is nearly done.
You've given all, you've done your best,
By every measure, you have won!

It Takes a Village to Race a Runner

My first attempt at a Boston Qualifier (BQ) was at the Medtronic Twin Cities Marathon in 2008. I was working at a running shoe store and was swept up in the fervor of marathoning by customers, friends and family members that either ran marathons or wanted to run marathons. I quickly discovered this support system was the elixir that would keep my motivation fueled for the next eight years during my quest to BQ.

For some, motivation may be an individual we run with multiple times during the week. For others, it's the weekend group run that keeps us on task. I ran for years on my own, however when I ramped up training and pointed for a specific marathon time, it was the training with and encouragement by others that helped me reach my goal in the fall of 2016 with a BQ -11:52 for my first Boston, 2018.

During the months of training before the race, I kept my village of supporters in the loop of what was going on, sharing the excitement of pre-race preparations to make sure they felt part of this historic event. They would ask how training was going, and I'd update them on efforts, successes and tough days on the roads. We'd discuss the course, my goals and even the city sights. Getting ready to run Boston makes it easier to get a conversation going because the race is so well known, but the support system needed for any racing endeavor is identical.

It's good to know that on race days I have people thinking of me and, in spirit, are along for the ride. I certainly think of them. I dedicate miles during the race for the effort and support they gave during training. Sometimes I crack a smile as I remember workouts that produced as much humor as it did sweat. Sometimes I need to hold back the emotions that come while giving it all you've got, knowing those closest to you will be excited about your race day success.

Whether it's the Boston Marathon or a local 5k, its part of the process to share your experience and thank those that keep you going throughout the year. I'm so grateful for their unwavering support and humbly acknowledge knowing I wouldn't be the runner I am today without them.

**"Running: I feel better, my work is better,
my relationships are better,
my life is better."
#RunningSavesTheWorld**
-BJSiddons

It's the Fall Season

Cracked off the edges of each day, it's difficult to notice the minutes drifting off as earth tilts just a bit. Summer solstice wasn't that long ago and yet today, leaving work at 5:15 pm, I was in total darkness.

It seems like just days ago I could leave my house before 5:00 am without a headlamp and enjoy a stellar sunrise as I made my way along the paths in Bunker Hills Park. Tee shirt, shorts and a cap and I was out the door to meet Dave for a run. Spoiled rotten, regarding prep time.

The trade-out, of course, is the post-summer season of Fall. Fantastic weather for running and racing among a landscape brushed with glorious colors that brighten our paths. We hold tight to the last, infrequent warm days of the year before they disappear entirely and the reality of where we are headed hits us with a big dose of certainty and a side of trepidation. Winter is next in line.

Like the deer, turkey and other wildlife in the park, we begin to change our courses as certain trails freeze up and become unsafe to use. Our winter coat becomes thicker, too, due to extra layers of tech-wear, hats and gloves. We slow down, but we don't stop.

Fall is a season when I work extra hard to be out on the roads and trails running, for two reasons. First, it's awesome. Second, without experiencing the gradual changeover to winter I am much less inclined to run outdoors in January and February, which means missing some incredibly beautiful winter visuals on my running courses.

As I set the alarm to meet Dave at 5:30 am, I think past the darkness and cold, knowing that once I'm out there I'll enjoy a great start to the day. And that's something I don't want to miss, no matter the season.

Rest Day

There's something extra delicious about an
early morning recovery run
following a late evening
tempo workout.

The alarm goes off and my running voice says,
"Dude, you get to run any easy pace you want today,
now get out there and enjoy it."

So I did.

A pre-breakfast shake-out run of four miles
with two side dishes;
the last bit of moonset glow,
and the early radiance of sunrise beams.

#EarnedIt

Upon My Return to Running

Upon my return to running,
Be it from a single, or
More complex, situation,
A few days off or
Months on end away.
I trust my heart will store
The feeling of humbleness
I carried within me.

Myriad small building-blocks,
Diligently laid out in perfect form,
Are the foundation of
Success for a long-distance runner.

Crafting each cornerstone;
Training, Nutrition, Recovery
As we load the trowel of
Life with all its elements to
Carefully fill in the gaps.

Bonding each section of effort
To the goal so earnestly
Pushed toward day after day.
First, in bits and pieces, when
Sooner than we realize,
It suddenly rises before us.

In stages, yes, always in stages.
Setbacks occur, compromises are
Made for the sake of the
Long-term relationship with a
Sport termed a lifestyle.

Careful not to wallow.
Smart enough not to despair.
Taking time for the essentials;
Repair, regroup, refocus.

Upon my return to running.
Savoring each stride, this
Delicious dance of
Motion and movement melds
Physical effort and
Soulful energy into such a
Contained excitement
I can barely restrain myself.

Upon my return to running.
My heart bursts forth short
Twinges of joy.
My legs fire signals of
Refreshed muscles to my brain.
My lungs carry the load, allowing
Potential hours-long runs
To nestle in my thoughts.

Upon my return to running.
I stop along the trail, mid-run.
Dwarfed by pines, sole human
Within the acres of my course.
Deer break across the path,
Blue Jay shrieks above.

Wind whispers between the
Branches that shade me;
"The journey, the daily steps
Leading to your grail,
That's the joy of running."

Upon my return to running.
May I never forget neither the
Trails I have run on, nor the
Trials I have run through.

Training Partners

My first week of marathon training is in the log, a total of 43 miles. Goal for the next four weeks is 40 to 45 a week, just getting in the miles and upping some of the long Sunday runs. Our group is excited about Grandma's Marathon, but as we begin to dial in our specific plans, it looks like we'll be breaking up a bit for some or our key runs. We enjoy running together, it's been a major reason we have all been able to keep up our winter training, however with each of us knowing that our time goals are different, it will take a bit of juggling to keep meeting on a regular basis, but we will do it.

Bryan, our speedster, has his marathon in May, and has the need for speed the rest of us can't support him with. Today he was able to train with a 2:32 marathoner and they ran 16 miles at 7:00 minute pace, hitting some 6:30's along the way. It was a great confidence booster for him, and a good benchmark of what all his training has been doing for him. Three months out and he's in great shape to begin his hill work, tempo runs and speed work. Fortunately, he will still run with us on some of his easy days, but I know he'll need to run a lot on his own in the next few months, as well as with faster runners, to get the training he needs to bust 3:00 on race day.

It's a cool thing, training with a group. We get to see the hard work of others, and hopefully ourselves, pay off after months of training. All for the love of the sport of running and the benefits it brings to our life, family, health and overall well-being. The empathy we share during the ebbs and flows of seasonal training help us pull each other through on the tough days and push each other on those days we are running well and enjoying a steady pace.

Running is a celebratory endeavor that is earned in a variety of ways. Some simple, some that take big effort. Like waking up early for a morning run, heading out the door after arriving home from a long day at work, or posting a great workout or race time.

It's nice to have a group to share those accomplishments with. We even get to share the tough times and help each other through those, too. There's nothing like the encouragement of fellow runners to help us realize that one race does not define a season, and that we will get stronger and faster.

On race day we are fortunate to have friends and family there for us at the finish line, but it's our training partners that really understand what we've gone through, that really know the work it took to prepare us for race day. And, however we finish, it's good to know they will be there for us once we've left the finish area and begin our training cycle all over again.

"I love seeing other runners succeed.
It gives me hope and fuels my determination."
#MyTurnNext
-BJSiddons

Grinding Out the Winter

Left work late and I've only got a half-hour to change and be ready to run with my friend, Fly Bry. It's winter, so I've got a lot to do.

Tonight's attire: Pair of shoes, pair of socks, shorts, tights, pants, long sleeve shirt, short sleeve shirt, long sleeve shirt, jacket, facemask, ski hat, liner gloves, gloves, Garmin 305, headlamp.

That's a total of 19 items, and I could have worn a reflective vest for an even 20, but Bryan and I were running on the auto-free trails of Bunker Park so not a requirement. Toss in a couple of pit stops while dressing, put on some lip balm and protective lotion on my face and I was ready by 6:20.

It's nights like these that keep us on task. We don't remember the effort of grind runs because the pace is below average, and you usually feel like a slug. Thankfully, Fly Bry was patient and didn't mind my slower pace, especially since the trail was fairly icy due to a rain-snow mix earlier in the afternoon. Oh, and let's not forget the 18' temp, a little more sleet and 20 mph wind gusts. Ah, winter in Minnesota. But a run is a run and it's 8 miles I needed for the week. You can't get through a long Sunday run on five-milers alone.

The tough days, whether they are done in the cold of winter or the dog days of summer, we get through them by putting our head down, focusing, moving forward, and finishing strong.

I love runs like the one I had tonight. It gives me a feeling of great accomplishment from something that, on a normal weather day, would seem quite ordinary.

And that's a good thing.

In Season

I'm sure Post Marathon Blues is a pretty common affliction, and certainly not limited to the marathon. It's caused by a training and racing season full of the very real psychological and physiological combinations that naturally occur due to the physical, mental and emotional elixir running delivers to the body, mind and soul. Whether the concoction is mixed for 5k speed or marathon endurance, it's an addictive potion that's hard to replace once the season is over.

Staying "in season" too long isn't a great idea for every runner. Resting spells and recovery gaps clean out the system and let the anguish of hill workouts, intervals and multiple hour runs drain from your muscle memory, one easy run day after another. This slow leak of the previous season's workouts drips with scar tissue, mad sprints and long drives to the finish line. Natural healing at its finest.

It's not by chance our running seasons coincide with those provided by Mother Nature. Spring is rebirth, fresh legs and the craving for speed, speed, speed! We break out of the winter months with high hopes and tempered anxiety for the magical season that has us circling the track with a gravitational pull that rivals Earth's own circuit around the sun.

Summer finds us sweating profusely to cleanse ourselves of not only weight but the cobwebs of life's daily routines, in favor of a group run or solo effort in the mad heat of mid-July. It's base building season and we look past the heat mirage floating on the road ahead and trust ourselves to deliver a fall running-season-reality that is more fitness than fantasy. We put in the time to deliver us from the evil that goes by the name of 'Undertrained'.

And then we are back to the future, another fall road-racing season behind for most of us, yet some of the lucky ones partake in Championship Season. It's for the young and the restless, but Championship Season is the part of our running culture that brings headlines to the sport. Even for us citizen runners, we need to know the sport is expanding. It's a living and breathing entity full of talented, hard-working runners that continue to push the envelope, whether they're local road racers or international, world-class athletes, our sport cherishes them all equally.

If we allow ourselves to keep the seasonal tradition alive and hold to the cycles of Mother Nature, including a restful winter training season, odds stay in our favor for a lifetime of great running, one season at a time. It's hard to be patient, to hold back and peak for just a season at a time when you feel like you can race all year.

You can run all year, be thankful for that, and remind yourself that winter, at whatever level it cools your region, comes for a reason. It refreshes and reinvigorates the world, just like it will your running.

**"Just because you can,
doesn't mean you should."
#StickToThePlan**
-BJSiddons

Six Weeks Out

Six weeks out, it feels like
Mile 17 of 26.2.
This is where the training gets real.
Injuries and illness
Humble our spirit
With torn hamstrings and
Infectious maladies.
The Grind stifles the drive
Of our daily motivation
Like the bitter cold of
So many winter training runs.

Five weeks out, it feels like
Mile 19 of 26.2.
This is where the battle rages.
Self-doubt seeps into the
Mind should any effort fall short.
Constant fatigue drains the
Nimble movement we so desire.
We have been participants in the
Runners Lenten season far more
Than 40 days, and we are frazzled.

Four weeks out, it feels like
Mile 21 of 26.2.
This is where the race is won.
We run through the brick walls
Of speed, tempo and long runs,
As so many have before us.
We stick to the plan.
Add miles to our bank.
Put in the training.
Do the hard work.

Three weeks out, it feels like
Mile 23 of 26.2.
This is where sacrifices pay off.
A strong finish awaits
Those willing to keep
To the plan, keep under control.
You are laser focused,
Determined beyond any doubt.
Charged with confidence,
There is no stopping the momentum.

Race Day.
This is where you lay it on the line,
Yet somehow try to savor and
Relish the effort, the experience.
You believed you could, and
The stretch goal was set.
You persevered through the
Bad runs and setbacks,
Were patient with
Recovery days, and
Humbly acknowledged the positive
Benchmarks of your effort days.
Suddenly, the miles are flying by.
You are pushing yourself just as
You dreamed, just as you imagined.
The last mile, filled with spectators,
Family and friends, pulls you,
Wills you, engulfs you with such
Spirit you transcend running.
You are the marathon.
The finish line, a gateway to
Your next journey.

Last Long Run Gone South

Like all good easy runs, it started off great. In fact, I had to talk myself into slowing down to keep MP+40 secs. Running the first two and a half miles through Bunker Lake Park was a breeze; dog walkers smiling and saying hi, trails finally clear of ice, life was good.

At the south end of the park I exited to catch another trail about a mile down the four-lane road. I had put on my 2018 B.A.A. 5k shirt for this section, as the bright yellow gave me a better chance of being seen, plus it helped psych me up to head out the door at 2 pm in the afternoon rather than get up early and battle the rain at 7 am.

Catching the creek trail just after 3.5 miles, I was sheltered by beautiful oaks and pines on each side of the asphalt path. I'm spoiled in that I have miles of trails to run without being near traffic, and I do appreciate it.

About the 4-mile mark I felt a bit labored. Glancing down at my Garmin I nearly freaked out at the pace. "If this is really 8:48 pace and I feel like this, next week is going to be a slug-fest." Within two miles I had gone from forcing myself off 8:18 pace to barely hanging at 8:48, then 8:59, then…9:05.

It wasn't so much the pace, but the effort it took to maintain. My Garmin is pretty old, bought on-line as 'refurbished'. It has served me well but lately seems to be fading like a runner that went out way too fast. I started thinking it was the watch…it couldn't be me. And then, maybe it was the Perkins skillet breakfast I had eaten four hours earlier, I never run after breakfast.

The pace kept getting slower as I tried to maintain… *"Garmin! Gaaarmiiiin!! What are you doing? This can't be the right pace. Are you mad at me for running indoors at the Y all winter? Is that what this is all about?"*

A year's long relationship with my GPS was deteriorating right before my eyes... *"Gaaaarrrmiiiiiin! It was such a tough Minnesota winter. I had to train indoors, I had to."* I kept looking at my watch until, finally, I knew I had to go it alone without worrying about the pace.

I'm nine days out from Boston feeling like crap, I thought. A wayward runner six miles from home. No phone, the fountain at the park is under construction so no mid-run water, and it could start raining at any minute. Heading back, I pulled the one GU packet from my shorts and took my time taking it in. Funny, about the same place where the wheels fell off on the way out, I started to feel better. GU to the rescue.

I knew the smart thing to do was just cruise back, and that's what I did. Taking what the day gave me, and realizing the hay was in the barn helped me relax. Trying to fight this run would be like trying to rearrange the hay with no gain in storage space; the only thing that could happen would be for the hay bales to tumble onto me, trapping me on the straw-filled barn floor among the manure and mice.

As I finished my run, I was thankful today was not race day, and I appreciated the heads up from my body that this coming week would be needed for plenty of rest before race day.

It's a fine line between being ready and being wrecked. We need to allow ourselves the freedom to adjust our training so as not to lose the race before it even begins.

"Tough runs help us appreciate the good days."
#RunThroughTheGrind
-BJSiddons

Patience. Trust. Fortitude. Courage.

These are the four parts of any distance race, especially a marathon. First, you must have the **Patience** of a Tibetan Buddhist working on a mandala sand painting as you hold back during the first five to seven miles of the race. Your body and mind will tell you to run like the wind from the second you pass over the starting line; "You feel great, go for it! Today is your day!" You cannot give in to this temptation.

Rather, you must **Trust** your training and "Stick to the Plan." You've put the miles into the bank, and today you must withdraw your hard work according to your pre-race plan. Cash in too early and you'll gain no dividends as you head to the finish line. Come crunch time, when everyone around you looks like a zombie, you'll be glad you held back and trusted in your plan.

Now, of course, it's time to put on your game face and call up all the **Fortitude** you can muster to maintain pace for the toughest part of the race. It's usually miles 15 to 21 when you need to fight the urge to give in and dial back your efforts. You must keep focused and battle through. Once you have a 10k or less to go, it's go time.

You may now allow yourself the **Courage** it takes to succeed. It's not easy to handle success, especially when you have put yourself out in front of others and committed the time and sweat equity into making this race count. Courage, it's about finding your path to break through barriers that have held you back in the past. It's also about gaining new experiences for the future.

Let go and discover not only have fast you can run, but how brave you are willing to let yourself be.

Potential:
The challenge of a lifetime
keeps knocking at my door.

Potential.

While tough to fully realize, we all hope to bust through our inhibitors and squeeze as much from ourselves as we can. Along the paths we travel, life choices are made, wayward directions are embarked upon, and parameters are set that inadvertently hold us back. Standards we will hang onto form around us for all to see, so we push our boundaries in secret, not wanting to expose true goals to others for fear of our possible failure. Hidden behind our best, no matter the level, is a desire for more, nestled in the harsh reality that we may not get there.

My running life has been a roller coaster ride on the Potential Train. As a high-school sophomore in the mid '70's, I ran times that showed potential. 2:08 for the half-mile, 4:45 for the mile and 10:17 for the two-mile. Unfortunately, the rest of my high school seasons were marred with running injuries and disrupted by a less than perfect home life.

I found my way back to running in my early 20's. Working in an athletic footwear store where there was daily motivation to run, my training became consistent enough to target my first marathon. Eager, but undertrained, I did what most virgin marathoners do; go out too fast and crash, tumbling across the finish line in 2:59.48. While thankful for sneaking in under three hours, I swore off marathons.

Roughly eight years later, my return to running marathons came in two options: "just to finish" and "pacing a friend". It was fun, and safe. It would take another 20 years before I would allow myself the chance to go for a Boston Qualifier, and ten more to commit myself to go to war in the battle of Potential versus Performance.

There have always been people that have supported and encouraged my running. I'm so much healthier in all aspects of my life, and they share in the better person I am because of the nearly daily physical, spiritual and mental rinse running provides. I'm so thankful for their support. After Jeanette had hit her first BQ, the bug infected me and I began what would turn into a ten-year quest to run Boston. It's easy to get frustrated and lose interest in getting a BQ, but I can enjoy the journey 100%, so my daily wins kept me from dropping the goal. I knew I had it in me, it was just a matter of getting the work done.

In 2008 I attempted my first BQ at the Twin Cities Marathon. It was a disaster. I had over-trained during the final six weeks, including racing a 20-miler a month out as my last long run, and racing a 5k the week before as a tune-up. Even though this was my 15th marathon, just like my first marathon I went out too fast. It was run-a-way freight train headed off the rails; I had to hold the drawstring on my shorts because all the gels I had pinned on were pulling them down. My initial pace was too fast, and I wouldn't slow down. Adding to the insanity, at about mile 9, a cold rain of big, heavy drops began to pour down on the runners. It lasted for over an hour and my body temp dropped as low as my spirit. My quads seemed to fill with cement. I finished over six minutes off my goal of 3:35.59 with a time of 3:42.08.

Three years later, in 2011, I was ready for another BQ attempt, again at the TCM. I was calmer, ready to go and ready to manage the race much better than in 2008. My friend, Bryan, #FlyBry, would run with me. We had planned to stay with a pace group, however what we didn't plan for was having the pacer drop out at the five-mile point. "I've got to stop at the port-a-potty," he said. "I'll catch back up," he said. Never saw him again. Not ready to run untethered, Fly Bry and I did our best to hit our pace with standard watches, no GPS.

The race became a lost cause of mis-managed pacing. Neither of us knew what our splits should be and the race ended with a nearly identical finishing time to 2008 of 3:42.18. Jeanette had a solid day and hit another BQ with a 3:54.41.

By 2011 my training group had gained a new running partner, Dave. Much younger than me, he soon found his distance legs and after his first marathon in the fall of 2011, was ready to not only train with me, but keep me focused for a third BQ attempt, this time at the 2012 Grandma's Marathon.

June, in Duluth, Minnesota, is a fickle time. Mother Nature came in with a typical hot and humid day in 2012. We knew by mile 8 it was going to be rough and I said, "Dave, I'm sweating way too much this early into the race." We were just two of the thousands that were battered that day, crossing the finish line nearly 5 minutes off our goal pace of 3:40.00 in 3:44.40.

Not wanting to admit defeat after Grandma's (it had to be the heat and humidity), we immediately made plans to try again in the fall. I was done with racing the TCM course for a fast time and instead decided to race Whistle Stop in northern Wisconsin. Dave and Stan, decided TCM would be their fall marathon. After our recovery from Grandma's we lit up the training and got ourselves all pumped for October. Dave and Stan turned in great performances at TCM; Dave beating our sub 3:40 goal with a 3:39.53 in only his third marathon, and Stan set a course PR for himself in 3:56.57.

Now it was up to me to come through a week later. Whistle Stop turned out to be the right choice, as I finally hit my first BQ. It was a cool weather day and a forgiving course (although mostly on dirt trials, which I would later realize is easier on the quads but slower on the feet). I struggled the last three miles, both physically and mentally, and felt I left some time out on the course.

My finishing time of 3:38.32 was 1:28 under the BQ, and with the then-recent changes by the BAA to have already reduced times by 5:59, I was sure I'd make the cut for the 2014 Boston Marathon. Sharing the success of my first BQ with friends and family will forever be one of my favorite days of running. I felt like I had reached a goal that was beyond my comfort zone and dipped into the effervescence of sweet Potential.

A funny thing happened along the way to my first Boston entry, which was for the 2014 edition. I was squeaked out by 6 seconds. Mission not accomplished. Potential not realized.

The sting of missing a chance to run Boston hung around like a sore hamstring. I buried it for a while but was determined to try again. The big carrot was a new age group time. I'd be 60 in 2018, and with a fall 2016 race I was confident I'd hit the time, but I still wanted a sub 3:40. Dave and I planned to test our revised training program, one that would build our late stage endurance, in the summer of 2016 at Grandma's. Stan, not being one to miss a race, also signed up. It was another hot and humid day with weather warning flags going from yellow to black by the end of the day. Dave and I revamped our race plan accordingly to account for the weather. Since this was more of a time trial than a race, we played it safe.

I've never seen so many fit looking runners strung out along a course due to heat and humidity. It got to Stan early, but he was able to hang on and finish. With a moderate first 18 miles and plenty of drinking at the aid stations, Dave and I were able to finish strong. We leap frogged each other over the last eight miles, "If you're feeling it, go for it," Dave said at mile 18.

We both pushed and, for the conditions, held up okay during the last miles. I was even able to put in a last mile of 7:40, and Dave came in less than a minute later, also finishing with a fast-last mile. Although my finishing time was 3:44.51, it was all about testing the training program. With a solid last 8 miles, we were very encouraged for the fall.

The October date for TCM 2016, if successful, would get me into Boston for 2018, at age 60. Even though I knew the last six miles of hills was not the best way for me to race for time, there were four of us running, including Jeanette, and I felt confident I'd clear the BQ with enough cushion to get in. The real challenge, the Potential goal, was a sub 3:40. Turns out those darn hills got to me again and I finished in 3:43.08. Not bad compared to a 3:42.08 eight years earlier, and good enough for a BQ -11 minutes. I had hit my goal, but once again, not my Potential. Jeanette earned her BQ -12 minutes, which is standard for her. Dave rocked the day and finished with a new PR of 3:30.02. In five years, this once novice runner had shown me what can be done as he had dropped his time from just under four hours in his first marathon, to the new PR. I was lucky to have such a solid training partner. Stan stayed steady after coming off an injury just one month out and finished at 4:00.39.

After chasing my BQ for eight years, signing up and running the Boston Marathon was not on our radar. I had attained the BQ goal that would get me past the second cut, and yet neither Jeanette nor I had a burning desire to run the race. Life was busy, and we had other running goals.

Over the winter of 2016-2017 we traveled to Huntington Beach in February to run the Surf City half-marathon, where I ran 1:42.54. In April, we raced the Goldy's Ten Mile, where I ran 1:15.16, here in Minneapolis. By this point I was in decent early season shape and the itch of Marathon Potential was creeping in. I had promised to pace my friend, Stan, at the Lake Wobegon Marathon in May, which would get my summer off to a good start.

Deep down I was setting things in place for an attempt at a sub 3:40 in the fall of 2017. To get me there I knew I had to do more than I had in the past ten years. I had to identify two of my biggest weak links and come to terms with them. It was time to come clean.

Following my marathon escort run with Stan in May, which was a whole adventure unto itself, I took some recovery time and then worked hard to be ready for a local 5k. It would be a speed benchmark for the remainder of my marathon training. On a warm day in early July, I was able to knock down a 21:04 finishing time.

I felt ready to head into a running schedule geared toward endurance training, as I now knew I had the speed I needed for sub 3:40. What I had to strengthen was Weak Link #1: the need for better endurance over the final miles of a marathon, and Weak Link # 2: the need to sharpen my mental game for the last six to eight miles. I had to find ways to physically and mentally push past the part in a marathon where the course is lined with the walking dead. "I felt good for 18, maybe 20, then it all fell apart," was not the refrain I wanted to repeat. Everyone feels good through 20. I had to find a way to race to the end.

I began to read and study what others had written about breaking through walls to maximize ones physical and mental abilities. I was encouraged and felt I just might be able to do this. My friend, Stan, also wanted to come back with a fall race, so we made plans to race Whistle Stop, the same course I had earned my first BQ at in 2012. I continued to frame up my training plan, and in late July, high on the 5k time and feeling good about my chances, I wrote down a complete, day by day workout schedule to get me there. Two days later, on an easy run with Jeanette, I pulled my left calf and would be set back for three months. Potential chewed me up and spit me out like a cottonwood branch through a wood-chipper. Stan wasn't far behind me. He had back issues pop up and had to scuttle his plans for a fall marathon, too.

With any setback there also comes time to sit down and eat plenty of humble pie, as well as an opportunity to digest said meal with an honest review and dissection of your running program. The good, the bad, the challenges, the hopes and the goals. I was nagged by past near-misses and yearned to join the club of wall busters, those reaching their Potential. I wanted to know the race effort I could give would be smart, well planned and properly executed to the best of my ability. I wanted to leave it all on the course without having it come crashing down around me. I wanted to reach my Potential for at least a day.

Now that fall 2017 was out of the picture, Stan and I set our sights on the Fargo Marathon in May, 2018. Fargo would be a new course for both of us and one we had talked about in the past. It was flat and fast, well organized and we heard great reviews from friends. Except for the wind. It's always windy in Fargo. Well, there's usually some kind of weather during a marathon, we surmised, and agreed to take our chances on Fargo. I had a new target date with Potential.

Shortly after Stan and I signed up for Fargo, my wife and I, of course, decided to run Boston 2018. Our friends and family helped us realize what a special opportunity we had in that both of us qualified in the same year. Jeanette had qualified many times, but this was my first chance to run. We chose to enter and run together, at a slightly relaxed pace, to celebrate our BQ accomplishment.

The only thing was, Fargo, my focus race, was just five weeks after Boston. How in the heck was I going to train, run Boston, recover and then race to my Potential at Fargo? Instead of worrying, I accepted the timeline and knew I'd be able to manage the training. I had to, there was no other choice. Reaching Potential isn't an easy task, I had to break new ground if it was going to happen.

Before my calf injury, I had figured that after racing a fall 2017 marathon, Boston 2018 would be my 25th marathon, and a good time to take a break from marathoning. I would have just turned 60, could focus on shorter distances for a couple of years and see what I could accomplish in my age group. All of this was conjecture as I was still dealing with a sore calf. I was excited about spring, but still concerned if I'd be healthy enough to finish Boston and race Fargo.

Looking back at my training log, I can follow the rehab I needed to get back to where I was before the calf injury. As we age, it sure seems like we get out of shape quicker, and it takes longer to get back to where we were. It was late October before I was able to push through a decent workout and feel like I was back; a 10k run on my own that I distinctly remember telling myself; "Run with fatigue." I averaged 7:53 a mile with a closing mile of 7:41. My body was ready to go.

Or so I thought. Four weeks later I was taking three days completely off due to a melanoma spot on my left leg. I was lucky in that it was a local, *In Situ*, skin cancer, meaning it did not travel. So, a nice gash on my leg (the doc did an excellent job, hardly a scar) that needed healing, meaning about a week of easy running. I'm thankful it was caught early and was confined. As runners, we spend a lot of time in the sun, it's important that we schedule yearly screenings for skin cancer.

At this point I was becoming a little paranoid that I'd never get to the starting line in Hopkinton, but once I got back to running after the surgery, things picked up. Workouts were coming together, and I was able to test myself a few times.

As winter approached it was time to head to the YMCA on a regular basis. Thankfully there were a few of us meeting there, including Stan, and of course having the luxury of Jeanette also training helped both her and I get to the Y more often.

One thing about treadmill running, you can really work on your mental focus. Over the winter months I was able to dial in on a weekly training program of five to six days running. It included Tuesday, Thursday and Saturday effort runs and two or three maintenance days. This kept me fresh enough to stay motivated, and consistent enough to see measured progress.

Tuesday was a progressive run, Thursday was marathon pace day and Saturday, whether at the Y or outside, was an easy long run. As the weeks and months went by, I was able to adjust times and efforts, and the physical and mental tools both benefitted. It was a particularly long winter, but other than a minor, three-day setback due to a sore instep, I was very pleased with the training. Potential was getting closer on all fronts.

As spring fought to gain ground on winter, Boston was quickly approaching. Fortunately, all systems were go for Jeanette and me. I told myself that bouncing back after Boston to be ready for Fargo would make me stronger. The plan was to treat Boston as a long training run, a very long training run, recover for a couple of weeks, ramp up for a couple weeks and then taper for about ten days. I was hoping the easy pace at Boston wouldn't take too much of a toll on me. I'd respect the distance and get back into training as soon as possible. Wow was I in for a cold, wet and windy surprise.

The now famous Boston Marathon Winter Monsoon of 2018 was a battle, no matter the pace. Jeanette did a fantastic job that day. We made sure she was geared up to stay warm during the race, since her low body fat could lead to hypothermia. Thankfully, the gear we dressed in worked out perfectly.

Keeping a steady pace and finally, heading right on Hereford and left on Boylston to the finish line, we conquered the storm! Even with inclement weather and extra gear, which after the race felt like a 25-pound sack of cement, we were less than five minutes off our goal time.

Finishing in 4:04:53, Boston is a memory the two of us will share forever. I'm thankful, and lucky, that my wife is such a studette. We celebrated with a finish line kiss.

I took four days off after Boston to recover. It wasn't so much the pace as it was the workload of running in the weather and wet gear. By the following Monday I was feeling pretty good and put in a nice 6-miler at just under eight-minute pace. The next Saturday, about two weeks post Boston, I did a 14-miler with Dave at 8:06 pace. The run felt great and we closed with a 7:19 mile just by stretching out the legs.

I was optimistic but cautious. Having been through enough training setbacks I was making sure to take rest days when needed, and ease back on the pace during some of the workouts. For now, it was quality over quantity. The miles were in the bank, and as my brother Al, (the person that got me into running during my high school years) was telling me, it was down to a matter of sharpening what I had developed over the previous months, even years, for the opportunity to maximize my Potential at Fargo.

Sharing my running with loved ones has always been what makes the effort worthwhile, and the pain during a training run or race more bearable. Jeanette, Dave, Stan and Al, have been the cornerstones of my running over the past years. They have always shown great support, as have my three children. They've been super motivating, have always listened to my concerns, and provided sparks of energy to keep me going when the flame seems to flicker.

I have gained much from each of them, as I have from others, but these are the people I think about most during the tough times of a race. They've been with me on the runs, cheered me on the good days and consoled me on the not so good days. They have seen me work hard, succeed at times, and fail at times. I'll never forget my kids taking care of me after one of the Twin Cities marathons when I was too cold and wiped out to move, and how much it meant to me. Without them there's an empty spot no run or race can fill.

As the reality of Fargo approached, I was beginning to feel the pressure to finally break through, to hit my Potential. I'd had enough of the 'Good job' races and wanted to do more, but I also held onto the knowledge that however the day went, I'd be okay. I'd have the love and support of family and friends that knew I had put in the prep work and no matter the outcome, they would be there for me.

But I was ready. I wanted this one.

It was about...damn...time!

Two weeks out from race day, marathoners begin to feel off their game. This thing called tapering starts and our training rituals are traded in for a succinct set of runs and off days we hope to parlay into a payoff come race day. After months of piling on miles and grinding through stress workouts, the notion of cutting back takes some getting used to. It's not like we can set it and forget it, our taper, that is. Each season, each marathon, can be different. We improve, we battle injury, we get older. I knew I had put in the work, and that I was in better shape than I had been in over six years, maybe more, so I had to be mature and accept the taper like a seasoned runner should. Ugh. There goes my fitness and here come the extra pounds.

There was one key run, an 18-miler, just before my taper that I did change, thanks to talking with Al. Before Boston, Jeanette and I were lucky enough to hook up with my good friend, Kevin, (a stellar runner and as entertaining a conversationalist on training runs as you're ever going to find) for a couple of long runs.

Kevin's group was a perfect fit. We ran the first-half together, then I was able to run with Kevin's friend, Todd, who was also training for Fargo, for the return miles at a slightly faster pace.

It was a real blessing to have those runs with Kevin's group. Post Boston, I was able to get a couple of solid 14-milers in with Dave, so I was looking forward to the final 18-miler two weeks out from Fargo as my last endurance test. Then I spoke with Al.

Sometimes we try so hard to reach our Potential, we blow right by it. We get close enough to grab a cup of success and we have about as much finesse as a rugby player in the middle of a scrum. It's easy to grapple in the mud, what I needed was a soft landing for race day, and Al set me straight. "The hay's in the barn. An 18-miler will take you two weeks to recover from, and that's race day."

He was right, of course. I had waffled on the mileage, especially after my key runs had been going so well. I'd trade in a slower, longer run for a faster, moderate length run. It turned out to be the perfect answer, a 14-miler at just under goal race pace that didn't tax me. It also allowed me the opportunity to come back the following Wednesday with a solid, hilly eight-miler at 7:38 pace with Dave a confidence booster at just the right time. Ten days to go and I felt like I was supposed to; In position to succeed and that's all I could ask of myself. I let myself accept the fact that race day could go well and tried not to let that weigh me down.

The anticipation during marathon week is always exciting, and this week was right at the top for me. Since Stan and I would be traveling to Fargo on Friday, I had a short work week for the Saturday race. Working hard to concentrate at my job during the day, not doing any crazy chores at home and trying not to think about the race too much filled my week. It flew by and suddenly it was Friday morning.

Marathon week is also the time to finalize race day plans. I usually have a few time goals in a marathon; A, B and C. I'll usually admit C and B to my running group, but A I hold closer to the vest.

That's the Potential, of course. The raw number that McMillan and Daniels charts say I'm good for, according to my other times at shorter distances. The number I have yet to hit. It's also about the same time needed to enter the New York Marathon as a time qualifier. Way out of reach, leading me to try for the half-marathon entry time, which I feel is closer to my ability.

Once I set the time goals, I figure my pace plan, which this time was a lot tougher. I announce two goals to my friends, "Sub 3:40, but I should be able to beat my 2012 BQ of 3:38.32 and be somewhere around 3:37.30". I print out a pace band for 3:38.00. Deep down I feel I can go faster, but it's safer to think 3:37.

It would still satisfy me to beat 2012, six years later, but what have I really got in me? Can I find the perfect pace between crash and burn at 22 miles, and red-lining it to 26.2? My race plan would get me to 20 in decent shape. Hitting my Potential would take getting to the finish line feeling strong.

It is always windy in Fargo. Race morning was cold, about 42', and windy, with gusts over 25mph. Stan reminded me that much of the course runs through neighborhoods and parks, so we should have a decent windbreak. I accepted that, and once on the course realized he was right. Sure, we had some tough headwinds, but we also had some side and tailwind. Dressed in shorts, gloves, winter hat, and long sleeve under a short sleeve, I was comfortable in my gear. It was overcast so I left my sunglasses in the car. I wasn't going to let the weather affect me. With the memory of Boston so fresh in mind, this weather was, pardon the pun, a breeze.

I knew I had put myself in position to physically perform on race day, Weak Link #1 was history. I was ready to attack Weak Link #2, overcoming the mental challenge marathons put me through from mile 18 and beyond. In the past I have gone into what I'd describe as a 'foggy state of mind' late in a race, and afterward wish I had been able to snap out of it, or not get lost in the fog at all.

The fog can hit during any distance race. It's that point when you should decide to go, and you just can't get clarity. Being able to fight through would be key to a successful effort. I had to, as Dave advised, "Stay in the mile you are in." I also had to stay loose at the start. I've been told I like to be social during marathons. It's true. I do like to talk for the first-half to keep me on pace and not go out too fast. It also helps me stay relaxed.

I needed to be ready to focus at Fargo by the halfway point, so it was extremely important to stick to the pre-race plan; 8:25 pace for the first five, then 8:15 for the next fifteen. That would get me to 20 with clarity, and then it would be up to me to remain in the moment and get to the finish without any major setbacks. There would be no room for excuses today, I just needed the race to start and let if unfold, hopefully, as planned. Stan and I wished each other good luck, and then the Fargo Dome exploded with fireworks to start the marathon. It was time to run.

Funny how so much pre-planning can go out the window at the last minute. Fargo happens to start inside a large, domed arena, a place where most GPS watches won't catch a signal. Hmmm, how's that going to work for pacing? I knew this was the likely scenario beforehand and was planning to let the GPS grab the satellite feed once outside. I'd run on pace and miles regardless of how close they were to the official race markers. Later, much later, I would realize how helpful it would have been to know exactly how far off my watch was for overall time.

One of my key pieces of advice for the first few miles of a marathon is to start slow, and then run slower. Having just come off ten days to two weeks of taper, marathoners feel great and have a habit of running too fast at the start of their 26.2-mile race. It's tough to control, however with a GPS watch you have no excuse for running faster than planned.

Although I ran by feel for most of my road workouts, on race day I was an addict for my GPS pace. I monitored it often during the first three miles and as good as I felt, held back to maintain the planned pace. At this point I was running with a few other marathoners and we were beginning to form a group. By mile five we were a bit ahead of the 3:40 pacer, just where I needed to be, and I was feeling very fresh. So far, so good.

Running easy, talking with Florida Guy and Bismarck Guy, I was appreciating the workouts I had put in and the rest I had taken. It was working. Still early, but my mind was already thinking of when to make a move. The farther I got into the race, the more I began to prepare myself for the inevitable clash of mind over body. If I was going to get close to my Potential, I'd have to steer clear of the mental fog that would want to roll in about mile 22.

As much as I had talked in the first-half of the race, the second-half was all internal focus. I had planned to get to 20 and see what I had, however, I also had a back-up plan of going at 18, as I had in 2016 at Grandma's Marathon. What I wasn't expecting was telling myself that at 16 it was okay to get serious. I worked my way up to a small group of runners and ran with them for a couple of miles, and then slowly pulled away. The course then meandered back into neighborhoods, lined with awesome spectators keeping the runners motivated. Lots of music, lots of cheering. I fed off the energy and worked hard to stay on task.

I was excited as I maintained my goal pace and freaked out when I put in a 7:44 mile around mile 20. It was happening! I had gained momentum by focusing on the mile at hand and was keeping mentally motivated by thinking of those that have been a part of my running. Miles were sweeping by and suddenly I was approaching mile 22, and in good shape.

As flat as Fargo is, there are some rises in the course. Nothing major, but they are there. One underpass comes in the 23rd mile. This year, combined with the wind, it was the one section of the race where I look back and ask, "Could I have been mentally tougher"? I had prepared for the fatigue; it was the battle royal for me and a key to my success. After coming up from the underpass the course made a quick right and put you right into the wind. It was a double whammy for me; the underpass took a bit more out of me than I had expected, and the wind was brutal.

I adjusted my running gait and headed downtown toward the Fargo Theater, watching cups and paper blowing across the road in a frenzied race to the other side.

Although I did not know my exact overall time, I was pretty confident my pace was under 3:38. The mile splits had been consistently under 8:15 all day, except for the first few miles, so mentally I was feeling good about the finishing time. While I was able to fight off the fog, there was a light mist I had to deal with. At two aid stations, somewhere in the miles between 21 and 24, as I grabbed some fluids, I took a few seconds to stretch out my quads. They were beat, as were my calves, however I knew from experience messing with my calves that late in a race can lead to serious cramps.

Maybe it was 5 seconds, maybe it was 20 seconds of stretching. I have always felt a few seconds used on fluids or a quick stretch can easily be gained back, however on such a day when everything was going so well, I look back and wonder how bad was it? Did I really need the stretch, or was I fighting internal battles to stay "In the mile" and keep my clarity? Whatever it was I shook it off and continued, promising myself that I wasn't going to stretch again.

The last two miles were all about getting the most out of myself and finishing strong. Striding along, working on meeting my Potential. I drew upon all the workouts I had done to get me this far into the race, telling myself, "You've felt like this in workouts, you can do this!"

I thought about family and friends and felt their love and support. I was working so hard mentally that my body just went along for the ride. Yes, it was physically demanding, but the mental transformation from being a runner pushing myself along the route, to a racer letting my mind embrace the experience, made the last two miles the best part of the marathon. I was feeling my Potential.

The Fargo Marathon finishes inside the same dome it starts in. I can't remember if I've ever raised my arms at a finish line, but for this one I did. Not knowing my official time (I had stopped my watch a few seconds late and wasn't sure how much I had to add from the start), I knew the day was a success if just for the effort. I had run the plan and the plan had allowed me to push farther and faster, yet not be crushed. I had avoided the fog, run past the wall, and put in a solid last couple of miles. Stopping just past the finish line, I gave a prayer of thanks to everyone I could think of, I hope they felt the positive vibes.

It's weird finishing a marathon with no friends around. I wandered about, finisher medal around my neck and a bottle of water in my hand. The post-race food wasn't very appealing to me, and I was starting to feel a little light-headed and queasy, not uncommon for me after a marathon. I headed over to the first-aid area and nurse Maria checked me in, read my vitals and gave me a bottle of Powerade. Ten minutes later I was feeling much better and made my way to the bag check.

While going through my gear I was struck with the thought of how fortunate I am. Married to an incredible woman and having three amazing children is my pinnacle of luck. Jeanette and our kids have taught me many lessons and continue to inspire me with the things they do and the way they act. As a running partner with Jeanette and as a youth coach for Jackie, Spencer and Harrison, I've had the pleasure to see each of them, on numerous occasions, step up and reach their Potential in sports.

As they have gotten older, I see their new goals reached in education, life partners, friends and careers. It's something I draw upon during tough times, and not just running. Their life experiences help me to be a better person, just as the experiences of other family and friends have helped shape the person I have become. The experience of one is shared by many.

Some say life is a marathon. We start out slow, cautiously finding our way among family and friends, jobs and careers. We work hard to maintain a pace we can handle and grow from, and still enjoy the many adventures life will throw at us along the way. Sure, there are going to be miles (days, months, years) we will need to grind through, and days we just don't feel like running, but the journey is so worth the effort.

The months of training, both physical and mental, helped me accomplished my A goal with a time of 3:35.41 and run to my Potential at Fargo. I finished nearly three minutes faster than my first BQ at Whistle Stop, six years earlier, in 2012. At age 60, I had run 25 seconds faster than my next fastest time, Twin Cities in 2001, and Fargo was my fastest since a 3:26.25 at Grandma's in 1987.

I earned my third BQ, this one a minus-19:19, in my current age group, and a BQ of minus-4:19 in my previous age group, the one I was squeaked out of for Boston 2014. It was a good day.

If life is a marathon, I hope it's one where we all reach our Potential.

It is possible.

"Crossing the finish line marks the beginning
of my next challenge."
#AlwaysMovingForward
-BJSiddons

Unrequited

Dislodged from my perch of focus,
purposeful contentment now unhinged.
I am loose, a shooting slab of shale
racing down the mountainside.
Unrelentingly fast, barely able to
grasp, as I try, unsuccessfully, to shake off
the impending, disastrous,
crash and burn that lies ahead.

The day, the race, broken into pieces and
scattered among the masses.
Drifting between gaps of hope and pride,
I'm wandering, then wondering,
the experience not yet fully absorbed.
Gathering thoughts form slowly,
like bubbled clouds before a storm.
Shaping and reshaping images and sounds, they
blur together into a hazy recollection of the
day that had been so well planned,
revamped, and detailed even better, for an
outcome that never came close to fruition.

Long months spent courting a marathon,
the most serious of long-distance relationships,
with gifts I earned and gave without hesitation;
Miles like I have never been able to offer,
surely bringing my goal within reach.
Effort days filled the motivation tank with
optimism, no matter the outcome.
Easy days provided time for reflection on
the journey that is distance training.

Tempo runs, at surprisingly strong paces,
were a kiss on the cheek, enough to
keep me going until my head or
heart asked for another to stay the course,
stoking the fire for another long-run weekend and
enhancing the vision of a successful race day experience.

Success is not guaranteed, and yet:
I invest miles in the bank with earnest.
I stay focused to remain on task.
I don't waiver and I stick to the plan.
I re-commit to the goal daily.
One lap, one mile, one workout at a time,
training shapes my days and owns my heart, while
providing much needed confidence as I
stretch my goals and expand my boundaries,
confirming to my inner self I am ready.

Pouring myself into training like
wine into a cask, knowing time spent,
albeit in the dark and on my own, is
soaking me with hope, health and humility.
My eyes see the physical progress,
my heart feels the emotional progress,
my mind understands the opportunity of
this race day fitness I must maximize.

Weeks before race day, I stumble mentally,
not knowing, not feeling it will all come together.
as the race of my dream approaches, I look for guidance.
Desire turns to ask Honesty for the answer;
Have I done all that I can?

Race day morning held no surprises;
Car ride, train ride, bus ride, follow the herd.
The pre-race gathering spot is jammed, so many
runners at the ready and hungry to start.
Yet I am alone on this day, a solo marathoner
among the tens of thousands set to
run from Hopkinton to Boston.

Crossing the start line, most famous of all,
GPS watch beeps to life, it's go time!
Thoughts focused on my goal, imprinted into
my brain for months, I know what I have to do.
Pacing, so much concern about pacing.
I track my early speed, reeling in the
tendency to bank precious seconds while
rolling through the downhill sections.

Runners everywhere, pulsating energy
each step, each swing of their arms.
Tucked together on a two-lane road,
fluid form of runners bodies bobbing,
brings the road to life in vivid color,
trimmed at the edges with
spectators clamoring with cheers.
This energy pulls the runners, taunting them to
run faster, run harder, too early in the race.
Falling prey to the well-meaning fans will only
bring runners pain and suffering later in the race.
For now, I ignore the encouragement.
Later on, my mind will beg for every bit of
support the spectators will throw my way.

As I settle into pace, I think only of
sticking to the plan, of proper execution.
Nothing else invades my thinking, not the gentle uphills
so early in the race that bandit pieces of my allotted time.
Not the silent assassins that crept into the race,
cloaked in diversion before I knew they were even a factor.
Overt in its simplicity, covert among my thoughts,
Heat and Humidity blanketed the course with an
invisible fog that would pull double duty.
Humidity sucking the moisture out of my body.
Heat cooking my inside from the outside.

My thoughts had been diverted for miles,
so much to consider on marathon day.
The sunny, sticky, assault by Heat and Humidity
hit me at mile 8, but did not register it's full
effect until mile 16, just before the hills of Newton.
I am wounded, but not done.
The hills, I tell myself, just get through the hills.

The battle is on, and I reason to myself,
do not overextend any further,
red line, and there will be no finish line.
Thoughts of a DNF float through my head, and
serious consideration is knocking on the door of options,
asking for a decision, which is quickly rejected.
Today will not be pretty, but today I will finish.

Pace slows, then downshifts again, I am
relegated to walking portions of the hills.
Shivers, as if chilled on a winter day,
come and go, trading place with radiant heat
bouncing off the pavement and the constant
feeling of running inside a greenhouse.
Signals alerting me my body is in overdrive trying to
cool off, to regulate, to inform my mind;
Something is not right.

Aid-station to aid-station is my strategy to survive.
I accept my fate and peel away pride all the way
down to my most humble running self.
Volunteers are my First Responders,
handing me cups of elixir to refresh my low levels and
keep the motor running, their encouragement as
important as the carbs and electrolytes I gulp down.
Watering my head with a full cup of water, at times
so cold it takes my breath away. I pour a second on
my neck and back, sometimes a third upon my quads.
Passing runners, being passed my many, I know the
fate of others is also tough, some much worse off.
I pray for myself, I pray for them, I pray to get to the finish.

Paying homage to the course, the race, the history
that is Boston, I resolve to make it up Heartbreak Hill
without a stop. It is slow, it is painful, it is accomplished.
I am encouraged, my spirit is lifted, and the downhill that
follows brings me new hope that the day will see me
cross the line I have come to honor. I begin to ride the
emotional roller-coaster that is a combination of
Gratefulness, Happiness, Joy and Thanks. And
Pain, lots of pain to remind me life can change in an instant.

Along the remainder of the course, the
runner's mood is one of high anticipation.
Knowing the finish line is near, participants and
spectators sense the coming excitement of
Right on Hereford, Left on Boylston.
You see those that can, begin to pick up their pace,
others show a resolve not to slow down, to stay steady.
Spectators are more encouraging now than ever, and
There is more to come.

At the sighting of the Citgo sign,
hearts are lifted, even mine.
I cross a street patterned with cobblestone and
nearly twist my ankle not more than a
mile and a half from the finish.
Slowing, re-grouping,
I steady myself and draw upon the crowd for support.
They do not let me down, they are incredible.

Under the blue one-mile overpass,
Boston Strong in bold gold.
I am so close, I am soaking up the
last miles as if I may never be back.
I turn to the crowd
as I come up from the last underpass, and
show my B.A.A. 5k shirt, it's logo universally known.
They cheer for me and I am lifted again,
I am going to do this!

As I turn right on Hereford,
the buildings guide runners to the
hallowed left on Boylston,
and the sidewalks are packed with
the best race fans I have ever encountered.
Goosebumps run up and down my arms, I am floating now,
ready for the finish I look around and take in the moment.

Rounding the corner, onto Boylston, I feel as if in a dream.
Cheers from the thousands of spectators
bounce from side to side,
Historical buildings taking in another year of
Boston Marathon finishers,
reverberating the new and
old spirits that have passed this way before.
The rush is intoxicating,
I am on a runners high like no other.

I slow my pace, I let my mind
imprint these moments to savor another day.
To bring me back to this exact moment,
this euphoria that is Boston on Boylston.

Nearly to the finish,
I look for the monument.
2013 will forever live and
never be forgotten.
I slow to a walk as I pass the monument,
hand over my heart.
In 2012, I was a week away from
running Boston in 2013, I wonder;
Would my family have been standing there that day?

Once again on my way, emotions get the best of me.
Tears form at the edges of my eyes, the glossy view even
more overwhelming, more meaningful.
Over the line and I stop as soon as possible,
not a step extra today.

Grateful, thankful,
not yet able to understand
the many lessons taught to me this day.
I will be better for the experience,
yet it will be many weeks to fully appreciate
the race,
the battle,
the opportunity to know defeat and
the desire to rise again to
the challenge that is the Marathon.

Ode to One Last Race

Farther down the trail,
My leg strength fading,
Lung capacity diminished,
And heart losing muscle.
It will be time,
For a time,
One last time.

How will I choose,
A final finish line,
That ends more than the race?
To embrace,
To relish,
To sear upon my mind.
For a time,
One last time.

With nary a chance to lose,
For completion brings a win,
I'll sift through years of memories.
Of trials and trails,
Of tears and smiles,
Of fondness for my friends,
To select a special day.
For a time,
One last time.

My recall will, undoubtedly,
Bring to mind my favorite,
Places,
Paces,
Races,
And faces.
I'll struggle like all distance runners,
Grinding through the toughest miles.
Hanging on until the perfect course,
Fills my heart and leaves no doubt,
Where I'll start,
To say goodbye.

Be it then of no surprise,
Nor even a hint of dismay,
Certainly, the final path,
Must begin out Hopkinton way.

For Gabe

Swift were her times,
Around the oval,
On the roads,
Down the trails.

Yet never too rushed to
Talk, to Hug, to
Listen, to Encourage.

Time generously shared with
Those she didn't know.
Time lovingly savored
With family and friends.
Time battling fiercely against the
Clock and competition.
Time etched forever into
The heart of her love.

How one, so fleet of foot,
Impacted and inspired,
With kindness in her voice,
With joy in her spirit,
With courage in her drive,
So many, So quickly,
So honestly.

Lucky are we,
To have known her,
To have known of her.
Life's cruel irony
Played out with grace,
Gabe's never-ending story;
So fast, So soon,
So amazing.

P.S.

I don't know where the fountain of ideas flows from for writing, but I am very grateful my words continue to stream forth.

Moving someone to comment or to express emotion after reading one of my pieces is what keeps me writing.

I love to write and am thankful you read this book. My hope is that along the way there were passages that moved you and connected with you, runner or non-runner, as they did with me when I wrote them.

This journey we are on travels different paths for each of us. May yours be one marked with plenty of joy and promise, fulfillment and accomplishments.

Most of all, may your journey be with those at your side you love the most, be it for a few hours, many days, or if truly blessed, dozens of years.

Life is short. Run long.

Brian

Also written
by
Brian James Siddons

The Voyageurs:
Discovery in Havenswood Valley

About the Author

Brian James Siddons

Born and raised in Southern California, Brian has been running since the summer of 1972, when his older brother, Al, talked him and his friend, Tom, into trying a two-mile cross-country race at Griffith Park, in Los Angeles. That was just before the start of his freshman year in high school and he's been running ever since. Brian's lifelong passion for writing was the perfect pairing to produce this anthology.

Living in Minnesota since 1986, a fantastic place to run and write, Brian is married to Jeanette, with whom they have three amazing children; Jackie, Spencer and Harrison.

**"To run is to express yourself through movement.
Be the artist that you are!"
#PaintThePicture**
-BJSiddons

Made in the
USA
Lexington, KY

54690307R00074